Medical Law in Turkey

Medical Law in Turkey

Fifth Edition

Gürkan Sert
Şefik Görkey

This book was originally published as a monograph in the International Encyclopaedia of Laws/Medical Law.

Founding Editor: Roger Blanpain
General Editor: Frank Hendrickx
Volume Editor: Herman Nys; Associate Editor: Tom Goffin

Wolters Kluwer

Published by:
Kluwer Law International B.V.
PO Box 316
2400 AH Alphen aan den Rijn
The Netherlands
E-mail: lrs-sales@wolterskluwer.com
Website: www.wolterskluwer.com/en/solutions/kluwerlawinternational

Sold and distributed by:
Wolters Kluwer Legal & Regulatory U.S.
920 Links Avenue
Landisville, PA 17538
United States of America
E-mail: customer.service@wolterskluwer.com

ISBN 978-94-035-2346-0

e-Book: ISBN 978-94-035-2636-2
web-PDF: ISBN 978-94-035-2646-1

This title is available on www.kluwerlawonline.com

The Authors

Gürkan Sert was born on 12 April 1975, and he graduated from Marmara University, Faculty of Law in 1999. He started studying with Professor Şefik Görkey in Marmara University, Faculty of Medicine, Department of Medical Ethics and History of Medicine, and he obtained his Master's for his thesis on patient rights in 2003. He started as a lecturer in the same department in 2004 and received his doctoral degree for his thesis on *Privacy in Healthcare Service* in 2007. Sert has published his first book *Hasta Hakları – Uluslararası Bildirgeler ve Tıp Etiği Açısından* (*Patient Rights from the Perspective of International Documents and Medical Ethics*) in 2004, and his next book on privacy and confidentiality of private life in healthcare service in 2008. In the following years, Gürkan Sert's books on 'reproductive rights' and 'medical law' were published. He has also written a chapter in a book on the ethical review of animal research. He has published articles on the legal liability of the physicians, reproductive rights, patients' rights and rights of HIV (+) individuals. Gürkan Sert is a member of the clinical research ethics committee of Marmara University. He is the General Secretary of the Turkish Bioethics Association. 'In addition, he has extensive experience as an educator; he has served both as an instructor and as a counsellor in several education projects on patient rights and reproductive rights conducted by non-governmental organizations. Between October 2018 and September 2019, he worked as a visiting Professor at the John Dossettor Health Ethics Center of the Faculty of Medicine and Dentistry at Alberta University (Canada). He is currently the Head of the Department of Medical History and Ethics at Marmara University Faculty of Medicine.

The Authors

Şefik Görkey was born on 24 April 1961, and he graduated from Istanbul University, Faculty of Dentistry in 1985 and received his doctoral degree in 1989 in Medical History and Ethics. He started lecturing in the Faculty of Medicine, Marmara University, Turkey, in 1993 as the founder of the Department of Medical Ethics and History of Medicine. He was appointed as Professor in 1999. He lectured in Marmara University, Medical History and Ethics Department until 2021 and he is currently the Chair and founder of Koç University, History of Medicine and Ethics Department. Görkey has published in the field of medical ethics, history of medicine, medical humanities and ethical issues in dental practice and research, and he has extensive teaching experience in the field of medical and dental history and ethics and medical humanities. He is a founding member of International Dental Ethics and Law Society (IDEALS).

Table of Contents

Table of Contents

List of Abbreviations

ART	Assisted Reproduction Treatment
ATR	Acupuncture Treatment Regulation
BBRRC	Bioavailability-Bioequivalence Research Review Committees
CEC	Central Ethics Committee
CHC	Community Health Centre
CRCB	Clinical Research Consultation Board
CRRC	Clinical Research Review Committee
DB	Disciplinary Board
DNR	Do Not Resuscitate
DUS	Test for Admission to Dentistry Specialty Training
FHC	Family Health Centre
FML	Family Medicine Law
GCP	Good Clinical Practice
GHI	General Health Insurance
HDB	Higher Disciplinary Board
LECs	Local (Research) Ethics Committees
LOPP	Law on Pharmacies and Pharmacists *(Eczacılar ve Eczaneler Hakkında Kanun)*
LOT	Law on Procurement, Storage and Grafting of Tissues and Organs (*Organ ve Doku Alınması, Saklanması, Aşılanması ve Nakli Hakkında Kanun*)
LPOMRA	Law on the Practice of Medicine and Related Arts *(Tababet ve Şuabatı Sanatlarının Tarz-ı İcrasına Dair Kanun)*
LRECs	Local Research Ethics Committees
MoH	Ministry of Health
MDR	Medical Deontology Regulation (*Tibbi Deontoloji Tüzüğü*)
PHA	Public Hospital Associations
PHI	Public Health Institution
PHL	Private Hospitals Law *(Hususi Hastaneler Kanunu)*
PRR	Patient Rights Regulation

List of Abbreviations

RAIHI	Regulation on Administration of Inpatient Health Care Institutions (*Yataklı Tedavi Kurumları İşletme Yönetmeliği*)
RARPAPR	Regulation on Assisted Reproduction Procedures and Assisted Reproduction Centres (*Üremeye Yardımcı Tedavi Uygulamaları ve Üremeye Yardımcı Tedavi Merkezleri Hakkında Yönetmelik*)
RCT	Regulation on Clinical Trials (*Klinik Araştırmalar Hakkında Yönetmelik)*
RDT	Regulation on Drug Trials (*İlaç Araştırmaları Hakkında Yönetmelik)*
RG	Official Journal of the Turkish Republic *(Resmi Gazete)*
RHCART	Regulation on Health Care for Assisted Reproduction Treatment (*Üremeye Yardımcı Tedavi (ÜYTE) Merkezleri Yönetmeliği*)
ROTTC	Regulation for Organ and Tissue Transplantation Centres (*Organ ve Doku Nakli Hizmetleri Yönetmeliği*)
RPDTOHC	Regulation on Private Diagnostic and Therapeutic Outpatient Health Care Institutions (*Ayakta Teşhis ve Tedavi Yapılan Özel Sağlık Kuruluşları Hakkında Yönetmelik*)
RPH	Secondary Regulation on Private Hospitals (*Özel Hastaneler Yönetmeliği*)
RPR	Regulation on Patient Rights *(Hasta Hakları Yönetmeliği)*
RPRHS	Regulation on Providing Remote Healthcare Services
TDA	Turkish Dental Association
TDAL	Turkish Dental Association Law
THP	Transformation in Health Program
TPA	Turkish Physicians Association
TPAL	Turkish Physicians Association Law *(Türk Tabipler Birliği Kanunu)*
TPHI	Turkey Public Health Institution
TUBITAK	Turkey Scientific and Technological Research Institution (*Official Turkish Abbreviation*)
TUS	Test for Admission to Medical Specialty Training (*Tıpta Uzmanlık Giriş Sınavı*)
YDUS	Test for Admission to Higher Branch (*Yandal Uzmanlık Sınavı*)

List of Legislations

The names of the Turkish legislations that have been referred to in the text have no official equivalents in English. Therefore, the English terms for these documents have been coined by the authors. Since different English terms may be used for the same legislation in different sources, a list of the legislations (with the original Turkish names in parentheses) used in the text is presented below to avoid confusion when comparing with other sources. Law numbers and the Official Journal *(Resmi Gazete)* dates have been provided when appropriate.

The hierarchy of norms for legislation in Turkish law also presents a translation challenge. The Constitutional provisions have the highest standing in this hierarchy, followed by laws (referred to as either Law or Code in the text) and decrees with the power of law. For legislation that has lower standing than laws and decrees with the power of law, the authors utilize various terms (regulation, by-law, etc.) in different sources while citing them in English. In this text, the term 'Regulation' refers either to a primary regulation *(tüzük)* or to a secondary regulation *(yönetmelik)*. However, according to the hierarchy of norms used in Turkish law, primary regulations, which are second to laws and decrees with the power of law in the hierarchy, have a higher standing than secondary regulations (if there is any) for the relevant issue. Among the regulations given below, Medical Deontology Regulation, Regulation on Medical Specialty Training, Regulation on the Practice and Control of Therapeutic Abortion and Sterilization Services, Primary Regulation on Private Hospitals, and Turkish Pharmacists Deontology Regulation are such primary regulations, and the rest of them are secondary regulations. Exceptionally, both the primary and the secondary regulations for private hospitals bear the same name and they have been explicitly labelled as 'primary' or 'secondary' for clarity. In addition, other documents which have a lower standing than regulations (circulars and directives) have been specifically addressed in both languages within the text:

- Decree with the Power of Law on the Structure and Functions of Ministry of Health *(SaJlık ve Sosyal Yardım Bakanliği Teşkilati ve Görevleri Hakkında Kanun Hükmünde Kararname)*. RG: 14.12.1983.
- Family Medicine Law *(Aile Hekimliği Kanunu)*. Law No. 5258, RG: 09.12.2004.
- Fundamental Law on Health Care Services *(Sağlık Hizmetleri Temel Kanunu)*. Law No. 3359, RG: 15.05.1987.
- General Health Law *(Umumi Hıfzıssıhha Kanunu)*. Law No. 1593, RG: (Official Journal*)* 06.05.1930.

List of Legislations

- Law on the Socialization of Health Care Services *(224 sayılı Sağlık Hizmetlerinin SosyalleXmesi Hakkında Kanun).* Law No. 224, RG: 12.01.1961.
- Law Ratifying the Approval of Convention on Human Rights and Biomedicine.
- *Biyoloji ve Tıbbın Uygulanması Bakımından İnsan Hakları ve İnsan Haysiyetinin Korunması Sözleşmesi: İnsan Hakları ve Biyotıp Sözleşmesinin Onaylanmasının Uygun Bulunduğuna Dair Kanun.* Law No. 5013, RG: 09.12.2003.
- Law Governing Compulsory Service *(Sağhk Hizmetleri Temel Kanunu, Sağhk Personelinin Tazminat ve Çalişma Esaslanna Dair Kanun, Devlet Memurları Kanunu ve Tababet ve şuabatı San'atlarının Tarz-ı İcrasına Dair Kanun İle Sağlik Bakanliğinın Teşkilat ve Görevleri Hakkında Kanun Hükmünde Kararnamede Değişiklik Yapılmasına Dair 5371 sayili Kanun).*
- Law on Civil Trials Procedures *(Hukuk Muhakemeleri Kanunu).* Law No. 6100, RG: 04.02.2011.
- Law on Penal Trials *(Ceza Muhakemeleri Kanunu).* Law No. 5271, RG: 17.12.2004.
- Law on Pharmacies and Pharmacists *(Eczacılar ve Eczaneler Hakkında Kanun).* Law No. 6197, RG: 24.12.1953.
- Law on Population Planning *(Nüfus Planlaması Hakkında Kanun).* Law No. 2827, RG: 27.05.1983.
- Law on Procurement, Storage and Grafting of Tissues and Organs *(Organ ve Doku Alınması, Saklanması, Aşılanması ve Nakli Hakkında Kanun).* Law No. 2238, RG: 03.06.1979.
- Law on the Eradication of Malaria *(Sıtmanın İmhası Hakkında Kanun).* Law No. 7402, RG: 11.01.1960.
- Law on the Practice of Medicine and Related Arts *(Tababet ve şuabatı Sanatlarının Tarz-ı İcrasına Dair Kanun).* Law No. 1219, RG: 14.04.1928.
- Medical Deontology Regulation *(Tıbbi Deontoloji Tüzüğü).* RG: 19.02.1960.
- Nursing Law *(Hemşirelik Kanunu).* Law No. 8647, RG: 02.03.1954, recently amended as Law No. 5634, RG: 02.05.2007.
- Obligations Law *(Borçlar Kanunu).* Law No. 6098, RG: 4.02.2011.
- Presidential Decree No. 1 RG. 10.07.2018.
- Primary Regulation on Private Hospitals *(Özel Hastaneler Tüzüğü).* RG: 10.01.1983.
- Private Hospitals Law *(Hususi Hastaneler Kanunu).* Law No. 2219, RG: 05.06.1933.
- Regulation for Oral and Dental Health Care Services *(Ağiz ve Diş Sağliği Hizmetleri Yönetmeliği).* RG: 14.10.1999.
- Regulation for Organ and Tissue Transplantation Centres *(Organ ve Doku Nakli Hizmetleri Yönetmeliği).* RG: 01.02.2012.
- Regulation on Administration of Inpatient Health Care Institutions *(Yataklı Tedavi Kurumları İşletme Yönetmeliği).* RG: 13.01.1983.
- Regulation on Assisted Reproduction Procedures and Assisted Reproduction Centres *(Üremeye Yardımcı Tedavi Uygulamaları ve Üremeye Yardımcı Tedavi Merkezleri Hakkında Yönetmelik).* RG: 06.03.2010.
- Regulation on Assisted Reproduction Procedures and Assisted Reproduction Centres *(Üremeye Yardımcı Tedavi Uygulamaları ve Üremeye Yardımcı Tedavi Merkezleri Hakkında Yönetmelik).* RG: 30.09.2014.

- Regulation on Clinical Trials *(Klinik Araştırmaları Hakkında Yönetmelik)*. RG: 23.12.2008.
- Regulation on Clinical Trials *(Klinik Araştırmaları Hakkında Yönetmelik)*. RG: 13 Nisan 2013.
- Regulation on Drug Trials *(İlaç Araştırmaları Hakkında Yönetmelik)*. RG: 29.01.1993.
- Regulation on Health Care for Assisted Reproduction Treatment *(Üremeye Yardımcı Tedavi (ÜYTE) Merkezleri Yönetmeliği)*. RG: 21.08.1987.
- Regulation on Medical Specialty Training *(Tıpta Uzmanhk Tüzüğü)*. RG: 19.06.2002.
- Regulation on Patient Rights *(Hasta Hakları Yönetmeliği)*. RG: 01.08.1998.
- Regulation on Private Diagnostic and Therapeutic Outpatient Health Care Institutions *(Ayakta Teşhis ve Tedavi Yapılan Özel Sağlık Kuruluşlan Hakkında Yönetmelik)*. RG: 09.03.2000.
- Regulation on the Practice of Family Physicians *(Aile Hekimleri Uygulama Yönetmeliği)*.
- Regulation on the Practice and Control of Therapeutic Abortion and Sterilization Services *(Rahim Tahliyesi ve Sterilizasyon Hizmetlerinin Yürütülmesi ve Denetlenmesine İlişkin Tüzük)*. RG: 18.12.1983.
- Regulation Regarding the Amendments on the Regulation on Clinical Trials *(Klinik Araştırmalar Hakkında Yönetmelikte Değişiklik Yapılmasına Dair Yönetmelik)*. RG: 11.03.2010.
- Regulation on Specialist Training in Medicine and Dentistry (Tıpta Ve Diş Hekimliğinde Uzmanlık Eğitimi Yönetmeliği) RG: 26.04.2014.
- Regulation on Providing Remote Healthcare Services (RPRHS).
- Secondary Regulation on Private Hospitals *(Özel Hastaneler Yönetmeliği)*. RG: 27.03.2002.
- Law on the Protection of Foreign Nationals Law No. 6458 RG: 11.4. 2013.
- Turkish Civil Code *(Türk Medeni Kanunu)*. Law No. 4721, RG: 08.12.2001.
- Turkish Dental Association Law *(Türk Dişhekimleri Birliği Kanunu)*. RG: 25.06.1985.
- Turkish Penal Code *(Türk Ceza Yasası)*. Law No. 5237, RG: 26.09.2004.
- Turkish Pharmacists Deontology Regulation *(Türk Eczacıları Deontoloji Tüzüğü)*. RG: 27.07.1968.
- Turkish Physicians Association Law *(Türk Tabipler Birliği Kanunu)*. Law No. 6023, RG: 31.01.1953.

List of Legislations

Preface

We, the authors, are very happy to prepare for Medical Law in Turkey. Unfortunately, Tolga Güven left the Project. He informed and got confirmation from the editors about his decision officially. We thank him for his contributions to the first two editions of this monograph.

General Introduction

§1. General Background of the Country

I. Geography and Climate

1. Turkey, known officially as the Republic of Turkey, or sometimes as the Turkish Republic (*Türkiye Cumhuriyeti*), has lands that extend to the continents of both Asia and Europe. Therefore, Turkey is a transcontinental (Eurasian) country that stretches across the Anatolian Peninsula in Southwest Asia and in the Balkan region of south-eastern Europe. Turkey shares borders with eight countries: Bulgaria in the northwest; Greece in the west; Georgia in the northeast; Armenia, Azerbaijan, Iran in the east; Iraq and Syria in the southeast. It borders the Mediterranean Sea to the south, the Aegean Sea to the west, and the Black Sea to the north. Turkey also contains an inner sea (Sea of Marmara), which serves as a landmark for geographers to mark the border between Europe and Asia.

2. The territory of Turkey is about 1,600 kilometres long and 800 kilometres wide, with a roughly rectangular shape. Turkey's area, inclusive of lakes, occupies 779,452 square kilometres (300,948 square miles), of which 755,688 square kilometres (291,773 square miles) are in Southwest Asia and 23,764 square kilometres (9,174 square miles) in Europe.[1] According to the 2020 census figures, Turkey's population is 83,614,362.[2]

3. Turkey's climate is Mediterranean temperate, with hot, dry summers and mild, wet and cold winters; however, conditions can be much harsher in the interior parts. Mountains close to the coasts prevent the influence of the Mediterranean climate from extending to inland, giving the interior of Turkey a continental climate with distinct seasons.

4. The capital city of Turkey is Ankara. The territory of Turkey is subdivided into eighty-one provinces for administrative purposes. The provinces are organized into seven regions for geographical purposes, but they do not represent an administrative structure. Each province is divided into districts, forming a total of 923 districts.

1. At http://en.wikipedia.org/wiki/Turkey.
2. Turkish (State) Statistical Institute. Figures in Turkish can be accessed from the following site: https://data.tuik.gov.tr/Bulten/Index?p=Adrese-Dayali-Nufus-Kayit-Sistemi-Sonuclari-2020-37210.

II. Cultural Composition

5. Turkey's cultural composition is a combination of Eastern and Western traditions, which could be described as a bridge between the two worlds. Turkish is the official language throughout Turkey.

III. Political System

A. Political System in the Republic of Turkey

6. The Grand National Assembly, which is the Parliament of the Turkish Republic, was formed during the War of Independence and accepted as the first Constitution of the modern Turkish state in 1921. The Ottoman Empire was dissolved entirely, and the Republic of Turkey was established following the end of the War of Independence in 1923. The 1921 Constitution was in force for a relatively short period of time, and a second Constitution in 1924 replaced it. The 1924 Constitution was in effect until it was replaced by the 1961 Constitution.

7. The last Constitution of the Turkish Republic was accepted in 1982, and it is still in force. Article 1 of the 1982 Constitution defines the form of the Turkish state as a republic. Article 2 defines further characteristics of the state and refers to it as a 'democratic, secular and social state governed by the rule of law; bearing in mind the concepts of public peace, national solidarity and justice; respecting human rights; loyal to the nationalism of Atatürk'.

Article 3 of the 1982 Constitution defines the Turkish state, with its territory and nation, as an indivisible entity and thus emphasizes the unitary nature of the Turkish Republic state.

8. The 1982 Constitution recognizes the legislative, statutory, executive and judicial powers of the state. These powers are independent of each other, and the Constitution emphasizes the separation of these forces.

B. Legislative Power

9. The 1982 Constitution states that the legislative power is vested in the Turkish Grand National Assembly (the Parliament) on behalf of the Turkish Nation and that this power cannot be delegated. The Parliament is composed of members elected by a general election. Under normal circumstances, general elections are held once every five years. The election is carried out under the general inspection and regulation of judicial bodies. Every citizen who is 18 years old is entitled to vote in the election. The election is based on a proportionate representation system, and 600 members are elected to the Parliament. Presidential elections are also realized in the same election every five years.

10. The Constitution provides a general overview of the operating procedures of the Parliament. The Parliament may legislate any law on condition that it is compatible with the Constitution. In addition, the Parliament may state its position on a certain matter by issuing a parliamentary decision. Following the approval of a law by the Parliament, it is submitted to the President of the State (President of the Republic). After the President's approval, the law is published in the Official Journal of the Turkish Republic (*Resmi Gazete)* (RG) and came into force.

C. *Executive Power*

11. With the amendment made in the 1982 Constitution in 2017, the head of the execution is the President of the Republic.

12. The President is authorized to appoint the ministers. The establishment, abolition of ministries, their duties and powers, organizational structure and establishment of central and provincial organizations are regulated by the Presidential decree.

13. The President may issue a Presidential decree on matters relating to executive power. The fundamental rights, personal rights and duties of the first and second chapters of the second part of the Constitution and the political rights and duties of the fourth part cannot be regulated by the Presidential decree. The Presidential decree may not be issued on matters envisaged by law in the Constitution. The Presidential decree cannot be issued on matters explicitly regulated by law. If there are different provisions in the Presidential decree and laws, the provisions of the law shall apply.

14. The President, ministries and public legal entities may issue regulations to ensure the application of laws and Presidential decrees concerning their respective fields of activity and not in contradiction with them.

D. *Judicial System*

15. The judiciary consists of independent courts in Turkey. These independent courts form the different branches of the judiciary system. Administrative justice courts, judicial justice courts, and constitutional courts are the primary examples of the system.

16. Constitutional review: There exists a Constitutional Court in Turkey. The most important task of this court is to carry out a constitutional review. The review includes the laws enacted by the Grand National Assembly and Presidential decrees. Constitutional law also granted the right to an individual application.

17. Judicial courts consist of first-level and higher-level courts. The first-level courts are separated into civil courts and criminal courts. The ruling of a first-level court may be appealed in a higher-level court. The High Court of Appeals (*Yargıtay*, also called Court of Cassation) serves as the higher-level court and is the last instance for reviewing rulings and judgments rendered by judicial justice courts.

18. The administrative judiciary system includes administrative and tax courts, along with the higher-level administrative courts. The rulings and judgments of the administrative courts may be appealed in the higher-level courts, which consist of regional administrative courts (bölge idari mahkemeleri) and the Supreme Administrative Court (Danıştay).

19. The Court of Jurisdictional Conflicts (*uyuşmazlık mahkemesi*) is the final authority to settle disputes concerning verdicts and the competencies of the justice, administrative or military courts.

IV. Population and Vital Statistics

20. As of 31 December 2018, Turkey's population was 82,003,182. Accordingly, 50.2% of the total population consists of men and 49.8% consists of women. The annual population growth rate was 13.5% in 2015, 12.4% in 2016, and in 2017. Turkey's annual population growth rate in 2018 was realized as 14.7%.[3]

In Turkey median age was 31.4 in 2016, 31.7 in 2017, and an increase over the previous year was 32 in 2018. The median age was 31.4 years for men and 32.7 years for women.[4]

According to the data on the child population in Turkey, 6,484,986 children were in the 0–4 age group and 25,608,596 children were in the 0–19 age group in 2018. According to the revised 2015 data, the number of live-born babies was 1,333,329, while in 2016, it was 1,309,771. A total of 51.3% of live-born babies are boys and 48.7% are girls.[5]

In 2016, infant mortality rate decreased from 7.2 per thousand live births to 6.8. In 2016, the perinatal mortality rate decreased from 7.6 per thousand live births to 7.2; the neonatal mortality rate decreased from 4.0 to 3.8 and decreased from 9.4 to 8.6 under the age of 5.[6]

In 2016, the maternal mortality rate was 14.7 per hundred thousand live births and it was 14.6 in 2017.[7] There are also regional differences in maternal mortality. For example, this is 7 for central West Anatolia, while 25.6 in the eastern Black Sea region.[8]

---

3. https://www.tuseb.gov.tr/enstitu/tacese/n-fus-verileri.
4. *Ibid.*
5. *Ibid.*
6. Sağlık İstatistikleri Yıllığı 2017 Haber Bülteni, Sayı: 6 28 Eylül 2018, T.C. Sağlık Bakanlığı Sağlık Bilgi Sistemleri Genel Müdürlüğü, 2018. https://www.tuseb.gov.tr/enstitu/tacese/yuklemeler/istatistik/27344saglik_istatistikleri_yilligi_2017_haber_bultenipdf.pdf.
7. *Ibid.*
8. T.C. Sağlık Bakanlığı Sağlık İstatistikleri Yıllığı 2017, Ankara 2018. https://www.tuseb.gov.tr/enstitu/tacese/yuklemeler/saglik_istatistikleri_yilligi_2017.pdf.

The crude death rate, which represents the number of deaths per thousand people, did not change in 2017 compared to the previous year which was 5.3 per thousand. Most of the deaths were caused by circulatory system diseases (39.66%). The second highest cause of death is caused by neoplasms (19.56%).[9]

Between 2017 and 2019, life expectancy at birth in Turkey is 78.6 for the total or overall population, 75.9 for men and 81.3 years for women. The average life expectancy of the 15-year-olds, the beginning of the working age, is 64.6 years. This period is 62 years for men and 67.3 years for women.[10]

Due to its climate characteristics, geographical structure and topographies, Turkey is affected to one extent or another by all types of natural disasters.

§2. General Description of the Healthcare System

I. General Overview of the Turkish Healthcare System

21. Since 2003, there has existed a transformation in healthcare services in Turkey named 'transformation in health program' (THP). Under this programme, there exist major changes in healthcare services, social security system and healthcare management.

22. Until 2005, health services were carried out by various public institutions such as the Ministry of Health, municipalities and social security system. In addition, university hospitals provided healthcare as well. In 2005, many of these service providers were connected to the Ministry of Health by law.

23. In 2011, the Ministry of Health organization was reorganized. In this context, Public Health Institution (PHI), Public Hospitals Institution and Public Hospital Associations (PHA) were established. Public hospitals institution, across the country hospitals and oral and dental health centres with opening, operating, checking and inspecting was on duty. Later, the name of this institution was changed to the General Directorate of Public Hospitals. In addition, working on specific issues, Turkish Pharmaceuticals and Medical Devices Agency of Turkey, General Directorate of Border and Coastal Health was established. PHI was responsible for the provision of first-step health services and social health services in general. PHA was affiliated with the PHI.

24. With this structuring, the Ministry of Health was more prominent in planning and coordination, while these institutions assumed the function of providing health services. This situation changed in 2017, and the Public Hospitals Institution and the PHI were abolished by a Decree Law No. 694 (dated 15 August 2017) and General Directorates of Public Hospitals and Directorate of Public Health were established.

---

9. *Ibid.*
10. https://data.tuik.gov.tr/Bulten/Index?p=Hayat-Tablolari-2017-2019-33711.

25. Primary healthcare services and implementation of family medicine: Prior to the implementation of the THP, primary healthcare service units consisted of health offices and mother-child healthcare centres. Starting from 2005, THP was implemented in pilot areas first and then spread across the whole country as of 2010. The main goal of THP was to formulate a general health insurance (GHI) policy that would cover all citizens under a single umbrella and implement the family medicine model. During this process, health offices and mother-child healthcare centres were replaced by Family Health Centres (FHCs) and Community Health Centres (CHCs), respectively.

The family medicine model, which is one of the main components of THP, is regulated through Law No. 5258, entitled 'Family Medicine Law' (FML) and enacted in 2011. However, during the pilot period of THP implementation, this law was first called 'The Law on the Pilot Implementation of Family Medicine' (*Aile Hekimliği Pilot Uygulaması Hakkında Kanun*). When the pilot period was over and THP implementation became widespread, it was renamed as 'Family Medicine Law' with Article 58 of Law No. 663 enacted in 2011 and the term 'pilot' was removed from the law text. Similarly, the details for the implementation of the law were first addressed in 'the Regulation on the Pilot Implementation of Family Medicine' (*Aile Hekimliği Pilot Uygulaması Hakkında Yönetmelik*), which was superseded by the Regulation on the Practice of Family Physicians (*Aile Hekimleri Uygulama Yönetmeliği*) issued in 2010.

Article 1 of FML states that the purpose of the law is to:

> determine the essential aspects of the legal status and financial rights of the health care personnel that will be assigned or employed in order to carry out family medicine services, which aim to improve primary health services, emphasize the delivery of preventive health care services in line with individual needs, to ensure that personal medical records are maintained and equal access to the services in question are provided.

Article 2 defines the qualifications required from the family medicine practitioner and states that such practitioners are either family medicine specialists working full-time or other specialist physicians or general practitioners who have received training as determined by the Ministry of Health. The same article also defines the auxiliary family medicine personnel and includes nurses, midwives and other healthcare officers under this definition.

26. With the THP becoming widespread, FHCs now act as the main healthcare service unit of primary healthcare in Turkey, as defined in Article 3 of FML. In accordance with the data obtained from the Turkish Statistical Institute, populations of all cities have now been distributed to FHCs. The same article also states that the Ministry of Health has the authority to employ specialist physicians, general practitioners and other family healthcare personnel through contracts. Accordingly, the Ministry cannot only contract with the already employed public sector personnel but also employ those not employed in the public sector (if required).

Due to low number of family medicine specialists, this transitional period relies on the physicians who are currently available. As of 2017, new contracts will only be offered to family medicine specialists.

Family medicine services are free of charge. If, however, the individual utilizes other healthcare institutions without the referral of her family physician, then she has to pay a certain amount as fee; the only exceptions are medical emergencies and mandatory situations. Primary healthcare services that are not a part of family care are provided by CHCs, and according to Article 5 of FML, these latter structures are regulated by Turkey Public Health Institution (TPHI).

27. Mobile healthcare services: Family medicine system also includes mobile services. These services prioritize preventive care and particularly house visits, follow-ups of pregnant women and neonates, vaccinations and chronic patients. Family physicians providing mobile services have to consider several aspects (such as the weather conditions, means of transportation and the number of registered patients for the family care centre in question) to ensure that routine healthcare services are not affected by these visits.

It should be noted that those residing in locations where mobile services are provided cannot be registered with another family physician for these services. However, in case they want to be registered with another physician, they can utilize the family care centre of their new physician. Under these circumstances, the new physician is not obligated to provide mobile care for these patients.

FML also refers to 'on-site healthcare services' that should be provided in certain community locations. These locations include penitentiaries, correction facilities, resting homes and orphanages.

FML also defines certain exceptional situations where the family physician may refuse to provide care for the patient on the condition that there is another physician available for the patient. Accordingly, these include unethical behaviour (such as an attempt to build a relationship for personal gain), deterioration of the physician–patient relationship to the point where it becomes impossible to deliver diagnostic and treatment services, presence of a judicial issue between the patient and the physician and presence of harassment, threat or similar issues which will not allow communication between the parties. This clause gives a partial right to the family physician to choose her patient.

28. Community healthcare centres: According to the Directive on the Establishment and Management of Community Health Care Centres in Pilot Districts of Family Medicine Implementation (*Aile Hekimliğinin Pilot Uygulandığı İllerde Toplum Sağlığı Merkezleri Kurulması ve Çalıştırılmasına dair Yönerge*), CHCs organize healthcare services for the inhabitants of its regions, provide preventive healthcare, ensure coordination between primary healthcare institutions and other institutions and conduct administrative, training and regulatory activities. In greater cities, one CHC is suggested to be established for every 100,000 individuals.

II. Regulation of the Healthcare System

A. *Law on the Practice of Medicine and Related Arts*

29. Law No. 1219 on the Practice of Medicine and Related Arts (*Tababet ve Şuabatı Sanatlarının Tarz-ı İcrasına Dair Kanun*) (LPOMRA) was issued on 14 April 1928. The law defines the legal standards of competence (the required qualification) and the standards for practising medicine and related arts for physicians, dentists, midwives, nurses and health clerks performing circumcision. In addition, Article 70 emphasizes the importance of obtaining consent for physicians and dentists and considers obtaining consent as a requirement that must be fulfilled before carrying out a medical/dental intervention.

B. *The General Health Law*

30. The General Health Law (*Umumi Hıfzıssıhha Yasası*) defines the provision of healthcare service as a duty of the state. The same law also recognizes the right to a healthy life and access to healthcare services for all individuals.

1. Fighting Against Communicable Diseases

31. The most important provisions for fighting infectious diseases are included in the General Health Law. According to this law, it is the duty of the state to improve the health conditions of the country and struggle against diseases and other factors that may harm the health of the nation (Article 1). It is stated in Article 2 of the law that the Ministry of Health is responsible for general health and social assistance.

32. The duties of preventing infectious diseases and epidemics from entering the country and the responsibility to fight against epidemics and infectious diseases in the country are included in the law. The duty of establishing health protection facilities, bacteriology laboratories and general vital examination and analysis facilities is included in this article.

33. Provisions regarding the establishment and duties of public hygiene councils, which have an important place in struggling with infectious diseases, are also included in the General Health Law (Articles 23–28). The council consists of the health director, pharmacist, military physician, private physician, government physician, veterinary, coastal health centre physicians, and the mayor. During the outbreak of contagious or epidemic diseases, they meet the governor, and the Committee gives information about infectious and epidemic diseases and informs the public about the benefits of a healthy life and protection against infectious and epidemics. The committee supports the implementation of measures taken when an infectious or epidemic disease occurs. During the COVID-19 pandemic, these boards took an active role in the struggle against COVID-19 as pandemic committees.

2. Measures That Can Be Taken at the Borders

34. According to the General Health Law, there is a provision regarding the protection of borders and coasts against epidemic diseases caused by international navigation and trade. As per General Health Law, in the case of certain diseases, specified in Article 37, at the land border, measures may be taken at the border for passengers and their belongings (Article 54). Measures include examinations of passengers, vaccination or serum administration, disinfection of items, isolation of medically suspicious persons, isolation and treatment of patients who have arrived by any means including train and any vehicles. In addition, the borders can also be closed if necessary prevention in neighbouring countries cannot be taken for the spread of infectious and epidemic diseases (Article 55). Similar precautions can be taken with regard to goods and passengers arriving by airline; for example, during COVID-19 pandemic, people arriving from abroad were screened and they were also kept in mandatory quarantine for a period of fourteen days.

3. Measures That Can Be Taken Domestically: Notification Obligation

35. Among the measures foreseen by the General Health Law for fighting infectious and epidemic diseases, it is compulsory to inform the authorities about the people who have the disease specified in this law.

36. The Personal Data Protection Law stipulates that health data can be processed and shared by authorized persons or authorized institutions and organizations in cases such as the protection of public health, preventive medicine, medical diagnosis, treatment and care services (Article 6). In this context, notification of communicable diseases is also in accordance with this regulation.

37. Many disease names are listed in the General Health Law, and it has been stated that the cases are required to be notified when one of these diseases occurs or is suspected or death occurs or death is suspected due to one of these diseases (Article 57). If a physician during his practice encounters one of these situations, he must provide the information regarding the patient's first name, surname and address within twenty-four hours (Article 58). If the address of the patient changes, the physician has to notify this as well (Article 60). The physician makes this determination to the sanitary office, and if there is no municipality or government physician, he provides it to the police or gendarmerie station. Police and gendarmerie are obliged to deliver this notification to the authorities without delay (Article 58).

38. The General Health Law obliges some people other than physicians to notify the patient (Article 61). Those people are chief physicians in a hospital, school and prison administrators, owners of factories, workshops, charity institutions, businesses, hotels, shops, pensions, inns, baths, tenants or managers, apartment caretakers, administrators in the villages. Those people are obliged to notify the cases of diseases listed in the law. The same article also states that pharmacists, dentists, midwives, caregivers, funeral service workers must also inform the authorities about the cases they learned during the practice of their profession.

39. The Communicable Diseases Surveillance and Control Principles Regulation issued on 30 May 2007 and the Communicable Diseases Notification System Directive issued on 24 February 2004, which were issued in order to regulate the notification in the law, were updated regarding the notification methods and the technical infrastructure of the notification.

40. According to the regulation, a surveillance unit should be established to organize notifications, follow-up notifications, and, when necessary, carry out surveillance studies for cases diagnosed with notifiable infectious diseases. This unit will ensure that information is shared and used within the framework of the laws. According to the directive, in order to prevent the spread of the disease in society and not cause social problems, notifiable diseases should be reported within a certain period of time. In order to make the notification made in a certain system, the procedure should be managed by the Ministry of Health (MoH).

41. In the notification system of communicable diseases in Turkey, rules were introduced to ensure a balance between public health and individual rights. According to the Communicable Diseases Surveillance and Control Principles Regulation, the personal immunity, material and moral existence and fundamental rights and freedoms of the person should be protected during the processing of personal data obtained through the epidemiological surveillance and notification system.

42. Notifiable diseases are clearly identified and listed in legal regulations in Turkey. Provisions regarding the diseases to be notified and their determination are included in both the Law and the Regulation. In this context, it is aimed to pay attention to the reporting of communicable diseases that threaten public health. For example, amendments have been made in the Regulation regarding the inclusion of COVID-19 among the notifiable diseases. Notification about COVID-19 is made within this scope.

43. The Regulation stipulates that the MoH determines national contact points in order to communicate with the World Health Organization and other member countries on behalf of the country in public health emergencies of international importance within the scope of the International Health Regulation. The overarching global framework is found in the 2005 International Health Regulations, adopted under Articles 21(a) and 22 of the Constitution of the World Health Organization.

44. Administrative fines are stipulated for those who act against the provisions of this Regulation.

4. Detection of the Diseases

45. According to the General Health Law, when an infectious disease is diagnosed or suspected, government or municipal physicians can investigate the presence of the disease by performing the necessary examinations.

46. The physician who diagnoses an infectious disease examines the reasons for the occurrence of this disease and informs his superiors. All state forces are obliged to support physicians who are working on this issue (Article 65). According to the General Health Law, the physician who performs these examinations has the authority to enter the house of the patient and examine the patient and other residents of the house in order to get information about the disease (Article 67).

47. Junior health officers are also authorized to perform these procedures. When an infectious and epidemic disease is detected, health officials must take the necessary precautions. All administrative units must provide the necessary support. Autopsy can be performed on a person who died of an infectious disease (Article 70). Compulsory death examination can be made for deaths occurring in places where there is a risk of epidemics.

48. Measures that can be taken regarding communicable diseases are also included in the General Health Law. In this context, serum or vaccine can be administered to patients or those who are exposed to the disease. People, buildings, furniture, clothing, and other items medically determined to be contaminated can also be disinfected. Domestic travellers can be examined and their belongings can be disinfected.

49. According to the General Health Law, those who are sick or suspected to be sick with infectious diseases listed in the law can be kept in isolation and observation by healthcare officials at their home or in units with specialized medical facilities.

5. Quarantine and Isolation Measures

50. Regarding the isolation of those living in the country, two separate regimes are applied. The first is isolation at home. The General Health Law allows home isolation if it is determined that isolation at home will be beneficial in case of diseases other than cholera, glanders and plague (Article 73). The second is compulsory isolation. Accordingly, patients with cholera, plague and glanders and people who are likely to spread these diseases will be subject to compulsory isolation. According to the same article, those who have a contagious disease other than these diseases, but whose isolation is not possible or sufficient in their places, will be subject to compulsory isolation. In this article, compulsory isolation is defined as the custody of the patients or people who are likely to spread plague, glanders or cholera under the security officers, in places determined by the Government, by banning them from any contact with other people. In order to take public health measures that will restrict individuals, the contagiousness of diseases has been taken as a basis and a distinction has been made between diseases within this framework. The abovementioned article of the General Health Law allows only compulsory isolation for certain diseases.

51. In cases where the patients isolated at home do not obey these rules, they are punished under the Turkish Penal Code for spreading infectious diseases. In addition, the regulation that will force these people to remain in isolation at the institution or at home is also included in the Turkish Civil Code (Article 432). According to the regulation of the Civil Code, it is possible to restrict freedom for personal protection due to infectious diseases that pose a serious danger. Within the scope of this regulation, a person with an infectious disease can be kept in isolation after the decision of the judge. Apart from this, there is no regulation to keep people under forced isolation.

52. According to the General Health Law, people with infectious diseases may be temporarily banned from practising their profession (Article 76). In such cases, those people and their families are supported by the state. In addition, assistance is provided by the state to those in need of assistance and to those who are kept under forced isolation and for their families (Article 83).

6. Forced Treatment in Infectious Diseases

53. According to the Turkish Constitution, a person's physical integrity is inviolable except for medical requirements and cases written in law (Article 17). The General Health Law has limited the forced treatment of diseases. These diseases can be treated without the consent of the patient (Articles 57 and 72). Since the General Health Law does not include a phrase such as 'and similar infectious diseases', COVID-19 cannot be included in the compulsory treatment.

C. The Law on the Socialization of Healthcare Services

54. The Law on the Socialization of Health Care Services (*Sağlık Hizmetlerinin Sosyalleşmesi Hakkında Kanun*), published in the Official Journal on 12 January 1961, aims to serve the purpose stated in its Article 1: 'The access to healthcare services, which has been defined as a human right in the Universal Declaration of Human Rights, will be socialized within the framework of this law and so that these services can be utilized in a socially just manner.' The meaning of the socialization process has been defined in Article 2 as follows: 'The socialization of health care services implies that the citizens may, through the premiums they pay and the budgets reserved in the public sector for health care service, utilize all sorts of health care service free of charge or by paying a partial amount of the cost.' With the emphasis placed on the provision of free healthcare service provided by the state, this law is considered an important step in ensuring a social state structure.

D. The Constitution of the Turkish Republic (1982)

55. The 1982 Constitution, which adopts a social state structure for the Turkish Republic, recognizes the right to healthcare. Article 56 of the Constitution declares, 'Everyone has the right to live in a healthy, balanced environment. It is the duty of the State and citizens to improve the natural environment, and to prevent environmental pollution. In the interests of the population's physical and mental health, the State is to regulate the central planning and functioning of the health services. It is to fulfil this task through the utilization and supervision of both public and private sector health and social assistance institutions. In order to establish widespread health services GHI may be introduced by law' and thus defines the limits of the duty of the state to assure the social and economic rights of the citizens.

E. Decree on the Structure and Duties of the Ministry of Health's Financing of Healthcare

56. This decree with the power of law (published in the Official Journal on 14 December 1983) is an important step which aims to provide the necessary planning for providing accessible health services to all citizens. Between 2011 and 2018, there have been major changes in the structure and financial responsibilities of the Ministry of Health. These changes are reflected in related articles in the text.

III. Financing of Healthcare

57. Prior to the implementation of THP, both the financing and provision of healthcare services had heterogeneous components. With the implementation of THP, these heterogeneous structures have been taken under a single umbrella. *See* paragraphs 25 et seq.

58. GHI is the insurance that provides protection of the health and financing of the expenses in case of health risks of every individual. With GHI, individuals fall under the guarantee of both *all public and private health facilities.*

59. Within the scope of GHI, services can be obtained from all public health facilities and private health facilities contracted with GHI. There is a premium payment basis to benefit from the GHI. Everyone who is insured, who works on his/her own behalf, who is a civil servant, who is voluntarily insured, who receives a monthly income from the institution, who receives sixty-five years of salary, who receives an honorary pension, trainee lawyers, who receives unemployment and short-time working allowances are covered by GHI. It is covered by GHI for persons who are not covered by any scope or who are not covered by the insured's dependants, i.e., unemployed, who do not receive income or monthly salary from the institution or who are not dependant. However, they also have to pay premiums.

60. In order to benefit from health services, general health-insured persons or their dependants pay participation fee. The amount of participation varies according to the nature of the institution being treated. For the drugs paid by GHI, participation fee is taken.

61. In the state of emergency, occupational accident and occupational disease, traffic accidents, maternity state, disasters and wars, strikes, state of lockout, compulsory notified infectious disease, treatments of drug addiction, individual preventive health services, children under the age of 18 and people in need of medical care of others, are free of charge as health services. In addition, private insurance companies provide healthcare services.

A. *Benefit from Health Services of Foreigners*

62. Foreigners with a residence permit or work permit in Turkey can benefit from healthcare services covered by private insurance or public health insurance. Those foreigners can be covered by GHI after at least one year of residency in Turkey. In order to benefit from GHI treatment services, they must have paid at least a month's GHI premium. Those people can benefit from the private insurance coverage, if they have a compulsory insurance in advance which is necessary for residence or work permit. Foreigners diagnosed with a chronic disease in a period before being covered by the GHI cannot benefit from the services related to the treatment of this disease within the scope of GHI.

63. Dependants of foreigners who are included in the scope of GHI can also benefit from GHI. GHI included in the scope of the foreigners residing in Turkey, which can benefit from GHI partners. In order for the spouse to benefit from GHI, he/she must not be studying abroad or being insured. Children of foreigners under the age of 18 who are included in the scope of GHI can benefit from GHI. If children are studying at high school or equivalent schools, they can benefit from GHI until the age of 20. Children in higher education remain under the GHI until the age of 25, unless they are married. Disabled children are included in the scope of GHI without seeking any age limit. In addition, mothers and fathers of foreign nationals who are covered are also included in the scope of GHI. If the dependant person of the insured included in the scope of GHI is diagnosed with a chronic disease before he/she is included in the scope of GHI, he/she cannot benefit from the scope of GHI in the treatment of this disease. All other diseases are covered.

1. Termination of the General Health Insurance of Foreigners

64. When the residence permit of foreigners who are included in the scope of GHI expires, their GHI is cancelled. In addition to this, GHI is terminated in cases when they are insured in another country, if they are deemed to be a GHI holder in another scope, and if they are deemed to be a dependant of the universal health insurance holder. Foreigners settled in Turkey without a work and residence permit can benefit from individual health plans or private health insurances.

2. Foreign Students

65. If foreign students who are studying in Turkey in a school or a college register within three months, they can be included in the scope of GHI. Those who do not make a request during this period will not be included in the scope of GHI during their education.

66. Foreign students who are deemed to have GHI must pay the annual premium within one month from the date of registration. GHI of foreign students expires on the date their education ends.

3. Asylum Seekers and Refugees Benefiting from Health Services

67. According to Article 89 of the Law on the Protection of Foreign Nationals, those who do not have any health insurance and cannot afford to pay can benefit from GHI for a period of one year beginning from the international protection application registration. The period may exceed one year for those with special needs and those who are deemed appropriate by the ministry to continue their insurance registration. In the law, unaccompanied children, disabled, elderly, pregnant, single parents with children, victims of torture, sexual, physical and psychological violence are accepted as under special needs/deprived category. All or part of the premium fee request according to their ability to pay can be claimed.

68. GHI is excluded from the scope of the person whose application is given a negative response by the administration. Foreigners found to have health insurance or have the ability to pay are removed from GHI. Notification is made to the GHI within ten days after the date of learning. Expenses of the treatment and medication costs are requested back.

§3. MEDICAL LAW

I. Health Law Legislation and the Sources of Medical Law in Turkey

69. Legislation consists of the Constitution, laws, decrees and regulations, as well as documents of international status. The concept of health can be defined as a state of physical and spiritual well-being of the individual. Therefore, health law legislation includes legislations and provisions that aim to provide the physical and spiritual well-being of the individual.

A. *The Right to Health*

70. To be able to define the concept of health law, the notion of 'the right to health' and provisions supporting this right should first be examined. The right to health is an important component of the rights an individual has over his/her body. In general, the right to health is defined as 'the right to maintain the continuity of a well-functioning organism and to demand the provision of treatment in case of disease'.[11] In this sense, the right to health has both a negative right (which implies freedom from the interference of the state) and a positive right status (which implies entitlement to demand service from the state).

1. The Right to Health in International Documents

71. The right to health has been given particular emphasis in several international documents, such as the Universal Declaration of Human Rights (Article 25) and the International Covenant on Economic, Social and Cultural Rights (Article 12). The right to health is also indirectly secured in every covenant recognizing the right to life. The European Convention on Human Rights, which aims to protect personal rights, has also indirectly secured the right to health by referring to the right to life in its provisions. Turkey is among the States party to this Convention and ratified it on 18 May 1954.

'The Convention for the Protection of Human Rights and Dignity of the Human Being with Regard to the Application of Biology and Medicine: Convention on Human Rights and Biomedicine' is another significant international document and is directly related to healthcare and medicine. This Convention also refers to the right to healthcare in a somewhat more direct manner, with a special emphasis on equitable access. It states in Article 3 that 'Parties, taking into account health needs and available resources, shall take appropriate measures with a view to providing, within their jurisdiction, equitable access to health care of appropriate quality.' The Turkish Parliament ratified the approval of this Convention on 3 December 2003 with Law No. 5013; this law was published under the name 'Biyoloji ve Tıbbın Uygulanması Bakımından İnsan Hakları ve İnsan Haysiyetinin Korunması Sözleşmesi: İnsan Hakları ve Biyotıp Sözleşmesinin Onaylanmasının Uygun Bulunduğuna Dair Kanun' (*Convention for the Protection of Human Rights and Dignity of the Human Being with Regard to the Application of Biology and Medicine: Convention on Human Rights and Biomedicine: Law Ratifying the Approval of the Convention on Human Rights and Biomedicine*) in the Official Journal on 9 December 2003 as Law No. 5013 and was enacted on the same date.

11. K. Bayraktar, Hekimin Tedavi Nedeni ile Cezai Sorumluluğu (*Criminal Liability of the Physician for Treatment*). İ.Ü. Yayınları, Sermet Matbaası, İstanbul, 1972, s. 16.

2. The Right to Health in the 1982 Constitution of the Turkish Republic

72. The 1982 Constitution of the Turkish Republic refers to both aspects of the right to health. Physical integrity, which is an important part of the right to healthcare, is protected in the second paragraph of Article 17 which states, 'The physical integrity of the individual may not be violated except under medical necessity and in cases prescribed by law. No one may be subjected to scientific or medical experiments without his or her consent.' Thus, the Constitution clearly states that persons cannot be subject to medical interventions and research without their consent.

In the third part of the Constitution entitled 'Social and Economic Rights and Duties', Article 56 addresses the demandability aspect of the right to health. This article secures the positive status of the right to healthcare.

B. Healthcare Services

73. The positive right aspect of the right to health allows individuals to demand healthcare service. This positive right necessitates the state to fulfil certain obligations, such as the protection of health and maintenance of the life of the citizens in a healthy status. Therefore, the state must take the necessary precautions, establish the required institutions and authorities and regulate them. Such duties of the state have also been outlined in the International Covenant on Economic, Social and Cultural Rights, Article 12, which declares, 'The States party to the present Covenant recognize the right of everyone to the enjoyment of the highest attainable standard of physical and mental health' and therefore these states should take the necessary steps for: '(a) The provision for the reduction of the stillbirth-rate and of infant mortality and for the healthy development of the child, (b) the improvement of all aspects of environmental and industrial hygiene, (c) the prevention, treatment and control of epidemic, endemic, occupational and other diseases and (d) the creation of conditions which would assure all medical service and medical attention in the event of sickness.'

1. Healthcare Services in the 1982 Constitution of the Turkish Republic

74. The obligations imposed on the state through the right of the citizens to healthcare are realized as healthcare services in practice. Article 56 of the 1982 Constitution of the Turkish Republic states, 'Everyone has the right to live in a healthy balanced environment' and imposes obligations on both the state and the individuals by declaring, 'It is the duty of the State and citizens to improve the natural environment, and to prevent environmental pollution.'

The term 'healthcare services' refers to activities that are necessary for individuals to maintain a healthy life. The Law on the Socialization of Health Care Services (published in the RG on 12 January 1961) defines healthcare service as 'the extermination of factors harming human health and the protection of public from such factors, treatment of patients, and rehabilitation of individuals with decreased physical and mental capacity'. It is important to note that this definition implies three different types of healthcare services.

The first of these services consists of treatment interventions. Treatment may be applied in outpatient clinics, at home or at the hospitals. The second type of healthcare service refers to preventive medicine services. Such service can be focused on the individual or the environment. The main goal of environmental prevention is to minimize or terminate the conditions that may pose a danger to human health. The third type of healthcare service represents rehabilitation efforts for physically or mentally handicapped individuals.

C. Health Law and Legislation

75. There are numerous legislative texts that regulate the provision, regulation and control of healthcare in Turkish law. The provision and financing of healthcare services by both the public and private sectors are defined in such legislation, and sanctions regarding the violation of this legislation by healthcare institutions and their employees are also included. There are also regulations on food safety (regarding individual and public health) and environmental health; such legislation should be evaluated within the context of health legislation. Lastly, Turkish law includes healthcare-specific regulations and several other legislations where only certain provisions are relevant to healthcare services. Accordingly, the scope of health law should include all types of healthcare-specific legislation, as well as provisions in other regulations that apply to healthcare, all of which ultimately aim to protect the physical and spiritual well-being of the persons.

D. Medical Law

76. The terms 'medical law' and 'health law' are sometimes used interchangeably so that distinguishing between these terms is difficult. However, it is important to understand that the scope of medical law is examined within the context of medical practice and the relevant legislation or regulations. Limiting 'medical law' with medical interventions will not be adequate to establish strict borders that separate it from 'health law'. The complex nature of the medical processes, the need for cooperation and rising costs have caused various professionals from different fields (such as insurance, food, and cleaning companies) to participate in healthcare provision. This situation has given rise to more complicated interrelationships within the structure of healthcare services and also modified the scope of the liability involved in medical practice. Determining liability within these complicated interrelationships requires the support of extensive health legislation. Therefore, it is more accurate to define 'medical law' as a sub-branch of 'health law'.

77. While treatment interventions make up a large part of healthcare services, there are also activities that are not medical in the strict sense, but are still considered healthcare services. For instance, precautions taken for food safety and for prevention of environmental pollution are not medical processes, but they are directly related to health. Therefore, health law regulates activities related to health and also covers medical interventions within its scope, whereas medical law mostly refers to legislation and provisions regulating medical interventions. In other words, diagnostic, therapeutic and other interventions interfering with one's physical integrity are related to medical law. Specific regulation, such as the Law on the LPOMRA, or Medical Deontology Regulation *(Tibbi Deontoloji Tüzüğü)* (MDR), that directly addresses physician practice can also be examined within the scope of medical law. From this perspective, 'medical law' focuses mostly on the legal status of the relationship between physicians and patients and between physicians and other healthcare personnel. In addition, the relationship between healthcare institutions and the patients they serve may also be evaluated within this scope.

78. Several topics, such as the concept of medical intervention, its legal basis, limits and scope, the liability of physicians and other healthcare professionals arising from such intervention and patient rights within the context of medical interventions may be examined under medical law.

E. The Sources of Medical Law in Turkey

79. There is no general legislation outlining a framework in medical law. Medical interventions are evaluated within the general principles of law. However, there are legislation, international documents and case law that serve as sources for medical law.

1. International Conventions

80. Article 90 of the 1982 Constitution states in its first paragraph that:

> The ratification of treaties concluded with foreign states and international organizations on behalf of the Republic of Turkey, shall be subject to adoption by the Turkish Grand National Assembly by a law approving the ratification. International agreements duly put into effect bear the force of law. No appeal to the Constitutional Court shall be made with regard to these agreements on the grounds that they are unconstitutional.

Similarly, in the last paragraph of the same article, the Constitution affirms, 'In the case of a conflict between international agreements in the area of fundamental rights and freedoms duly put into effect and the domestic laws due to differences in provisions on the same matter, the provisions of international agreements shall prevail.' Therefore, international conventions that have been ratified by Turkey act as a source for medical law. Provisions that may be relevant for medical law, such as those in the Universal Declaration of Human Rights, the European Convention on Human Rights and the Convention on the Rights of the Child, may also serve as sources of medical law. In addition to the documents listed above, conventions that include specific provisions with regard to medical practice, particularly the European Convention on Human Rights and Biomedicine (also called the Oviedo Convention), are among the important sources of Turkish law. The content of this Convention, which includes provisions on organ transplantation, assisted reproduction treatments (ARTs), and other general medical procedures are important in defining the legal framework that regulates medical practice in Turkey.[12]

2. Constitution

81. Turkish law contains a constitutional provision regarding medical practice, stating that the physical integrity of a person may not be touched without a medical necessity (Article 17). This same article also states that an individual may not be subject to medical research without his/her consent. Other articles related to the integrity of the body and the inviolable status of the right to life are also important for determining the limits of medical intervention.

3. Private Law

82. The general provisions of private law are the basis of medical law. For example, the Civil Code is of particular importance in determining the limits of medical intervention since it provides for the protection of one's physical integrity and the inviolability of his/her individual rights relating to his/her personal being. According to the Turkish Civil Code, a person may not give up such personal rights, thus forming a barrier preventing the refusal of treatment in cases of life-threatening danger. The same provision also prevents the individual from consenting to procedures that have no therapeutic purpose and threaten his/her health.[13] In

12. Biyoloji ve Tıbbın Uygulanması Bakımından İnsan Hakları ve İnsan Haysiyetinin Korunması Sözleşmesi: İnsan Hakları ve Biyotıp Sözleşmesi (*Convention for the Protection of Human Rights and Dignity of the Human Being with Regard to the Application of Biology and Medicine: Convention on Human Rights and Biomedicine*), Oviedo, 4 Apr. 1997. This Convention was signed by the Republic of Turkey on 4 Apr. 1997; it was approved by the Parliament on 3 Dec. 2003 and the Law ratifying it was published under the name 'Biyoloji ve Tıbbın Uygulanması Bakımından İnsan Hakları ve İnsan Haysiyetinin Korunması Sözleşmesi: Insan Hakları ve Biyotıp Sözleşmesinin Onaylanmasının Uygun Bulunduğuna Dair Kanun' (*Convention for the Protection of Human Rights and Dignity of the Human Being with Regard to the Application of Biology and Medicine: Convention on Human Rights and Biomedicine: Law Ratifying the Approval of Convention on Human Rights and Biomedicine*) in the Official Journal on 9 Dec. 2003 as Law No. 5013 and was enacted on the same date.
13. S. Helvacı, Türk ve İsviçre Hukuklarında Kişilik Haklarını Koruyucu Davalar (*Lawsuits on the Protection of Personal Rights in Turkish and Swiss Law*) (Mk. D. 24/a fıkra I, İMK md. 28/a fıkra I). Beta, İstanbul, 2001, s. 51.

addition, required conditions for certain medical interventions have been specifically addressed. For instance, the article regulating sex change procedures defines several prerequisites that must be fulfilled before such operations are conducted.

83. The treatment contract has not been specifically defined in Turkish law. However, it is accepted that the treatment contract must be compatible with the contract of mandate defined in Turkish Obligations Law. The Turkish High Court of Appeals has adopted this approach in its verdicts concerning medical interventions and evaluates the contract arising from the patient–physician relationship on the basis of the contract of mandate. According to Turkish Obligations Law, the person undertaking the work has an obligation to guarantee the result in the context of the work contract. However, such a requirement does not exist in the context of the contract of mandate. This is the main difference between the two types of contracts. Since the outcome of the treatment depends on many factors apart from the activities of the physician, it is not possible to guarantee the outcome. Therefore, evaluating the treatment contract within the scope of the contract of mandate is advocated by the Turkish legal doctrine and the practice of law.[14]

84. According to Obligations Law, the civil liability arising from medical interventions can be evaluated in the context of tort liability, as well as a liability arising from the treatment contract. The Turkish High Court of Appeals and Turkish legal doctrine have presented views that support both of these approaches.[15]

4. Criminal Law

85. Criminal liability is involved in cases where the intervening personnel have been negligent and the individual has been harmed. The criminal liability arising from medical interventions is determined within the context of the general provisions outlined in the Penal Code. In addition, the Turkish Penal Code includes specific provisions where the limits of certain medical interventions have been defined. There are specific provisions on organ trade, the unauthorized removal of organs and procuring abortion and sterilization procedures. Health legislation also serves as a basis for establishing the limits in the medical interventions mentioned above when criminal liability is concerned.

5. Turkish Legal Doctrine

86. Turkish legal doctrine also serves as a source for the judgments of Turkish courts. The field of medicine is a dynamic one, and it is possible to have topics that

14. M. Ayan, Tıbbi Müdahalelerden Doğan Hukuki Sorumluluk (*Civil Liability Arising from the Medical Intervention*). Kazancı Hukuk Yayınları, Ankara 1991, s. 53; C. Yavuz Borçlar Hukuku Özel Hükümler (*Obligations Law Specific Provisions*), Beta Basım Yayın Istanbul, 1996, s. 563.
15. M. Ayan, Tıbbi Müdahalelerden Doğan Hukuki Sorumluluk (*Civil Liability Arising from the Medical Intervention*). Kazancı Hukuk Yayınları, Ankara 1991, pp. 116–117.

have not been addressed in the current legislation. In such cases, different doctrines regarding medical intervention and its scope are considered by the courts when handing down their verdicts. Legal doctrine is also an important basis in cases where legal provisions are unclear or controversial.

There are no medical/health law departments in Turkish law schools, and medical law lectures are not routinely provided in either law or medical schools. However, in some medical schools, deontology and medical ethics lectures contain topics related to medical law. In addition, some postgraduate training programmes include medical law courses or lectures on health legislation. Currently, there is no association for medical/health lawyers in Turkey.

Part I. The Medical Profession

Chapter 1. Access to the Medical Profession

§1. Training Physicians

I. Access to the Faculties of Medicine

87. Currently, the medical education of physician candidates in Turkey is provided in the faculties of medicine. The number of these faculties is estimated to be around fifty and growing. High school graduates in Turkey pass a multiple-choice test (conducted once a year in all provinces at the same time) to be eligible for education in a faculty of the state or private universities. These candidates record their choice of faculty on the test form and are assigned according to their results. This is a centrally structured system with no additional acceptance process by the university; students compete to 'win' the right to be educated in the faculty of their choice. The lowest required score to enter a faculty is related to the number of students applying for admission to it, such that faculties that are sought after by the highest number of students will have higher entry scores. These sought-after faculties attract higher-scoring students and are considered more prestigious programmes. While only a small fraction of students are assigned each year, there is no official effort to restrict the total number of students who will be accepted to the faculties of medicine. In addition, the quantity of these faculties will be increased in the near future. This policy is not appreciated by the Turkish Physicians Association (TPA), which is concerned that the quality of medical education will be compromised with the growth of more medical training programmes.

II. Education and Training in the Faculties of Medicine

88. A full programme of education and training in the faculties of medicine takes six years to complete, upon which successful graduates are granted the title of general practitioner and may practice medicine under this title. The typical curriculum of a faculty of medicine involves three years of preclinical and clinical sciences, with an emphasis on lectures in medical/science theory supported by laboratory practice hours. The first three-year period is followed by a second intense three-year period in the university hospitals. During this second period, the emphasis is mostly on clinical practice skills taught throughout various clinical training rotations, including internal medicine, paediatrics, general surgery and gynaecology and obstetrics, as well as other branches of internal medicine and surgery. Medical students in the final year of the faculty are called interns; they receive few lectures on theory during this period.

III. General Practitioners

89. Physicians in medical practice are classified into two groups: general practitioners and specialists. General practitioners are those practising medicine after completing their training in a faculty of medicine and receiving their diploma in medicine, as mentioned above.

IV. Specialists

90. Specialists are physicians with postgraduate (or residency) training in a specific branch of medicine. To be eligible to become a specialist, a general practitioner must first pass a multiple-choice test (conducted twice per year) only after completing his/her graduate training in a faculty of medicine. The test is known as Test for Admission to Medical Specialty Training (TUS) *(Tıpta Uzmanlık Giriş Sınavı)*, which stands for the Turkish equivalent of 'Test for Starting Medical Specialty Training'. The length of the training period depends on the branch of medicine chosen. In addition, physicians eligible to join a speciality programme are required to complete and successfully defend a thesis in front of a panel at the end of their training.

91. The Medical Specialization Board was established in 2018. This board shall decide on the granting of training authorization and abolition of training authority of the educational institutions that will provide specialist training in medicine and dentistry. The same board is also responsible for determining the rotations of the specialities, to determine the faculties and training hospitals which are going to evaluate the scientific perspective of the specialist from foreign countries. These issues are regulated in the Regulation on Specialist Training in Medicine and Dentistry (*Tıpta Ve Diş Hekimliğinde Uzmanlık Eğitimi Yönetmeliği*). According to the Regulation, the specialist student who is enrolled in the programmes is responsible to do research, practise medicine and continue his/her education. The specialist student has the right to demand that the programmes be provided with the curriculum and standards specified by the board. The specialist student has to follow the deontological and ethical rules.

92. TUS is conducted at least twice a year by central/nationwide examination. Test for Admission to Dentistry Specialty Training (DUS) and Testing for Admission to speciality training in a 'higher' branch Test for Admission to Higher Branch (*Yandal Uzmanlık Sınavı*) (YDUS) are held at least once a year. To succeed in TUS and DUS, foreign language proficiency and the conditions of being authorized to carry out the profession are required. Specialization requirement is necessary for YDUS (Article 12). In LPOMRA, duration of speciality training is determined.

Pharmacists, chemists and veterinarians may apply for medical speciality training except for physicians and dentists. These people can be placed in the departments of medical microbiology and medical biochemistry if a quota is opened (Article 13). Foreigners can also gain expertise in Turkey. This person must be taken from the medical or dental school or equivalence to graduate from Turkey. They are also required to succeed in the Turkish language exam. Students who have graduated from a faculty with education in Turkish do not have to take this exam (Article 14). It is compulsory to request equivalence for people who educate in abroad (Article 23).

93. The training should continue without interruption. Those who stop training for any reason other than military service, postnatal leave or force majeure, and those who leave due to their own volition or actions cannot reattend the same programme. Beginning specialization, the institutions on which the students have enrolled are responsible for their education on legal and deontological issues (Article 16). After receiving training in accordance with the programmes specified in the relevant legislation, the students should submit their dissertation. Certificates on their specialities are registered by the Ministry of Health (Article 22).

§2. Manpower Planning

94. While there is no official effort to restrict the number of students starting the faculties of medicine each year, the assignment of physicians is regulated by the 'compulsory service legislations'. The efficacy of such compulsory assignments is controversial and is openly opposed by the TPA.

The compulsory service process, also known as 'the obligation for state service', is governed by Law No. 5371, known as the Law Governing Compulsory Service *(Sağlık Hizmetleri Temel Kanunu, Sağlık Personelinin Tazminat ve Çalışma Esaslanna Dair Kanun, Devlet Memurları Kanunu ve Tababet ve Şuabatı San'atlarının Tarz-ı İcrasına Dair Kanun İie Sağlık Bakanhğının Teşkilat ve Görevleri Hakkında Kanun Hükmünde Kararnamede Değişiklik Yapılmasına Dair 5371 sayılı Kanun).* This law provides the legal basis for the additional articles appended to the Fundamental Law on Health Care Services *(Sağlık Hizmetleri Temel Kanunu)* that describe the details of such service. These additional articles state that general practitioners and specialists, including those with a higher speciality training, are obligated to complete a compulsory service period for each level of their training (graduate, speciality and higher speciality). Additional Article 3 of the Common Health Law states that such service ranges between 300 and 600 calendar days, depending on the socio-economic development level of the district to which the physicians will be assigned. Additional Article 4 states that physicians are to be assigned on the basis of random selection (lottery), though candidates may state their choices as well.

Chapter 2. The Practice of Medicine

95. The practice of medicine in Turkey is regulated by LPOMRA (*Tababet ve Şuabat-ı Sanatlarının Tarz-ı İcrasına Dair Kanun*), issued in 1928. The law has been amended several times, with new articles added and other articles removed. Recent changes were made in 2004 and 2005, and other amendments for updating the legislation are also being planned. This law includes provisions that regulate the practice of physicians and dentists, as well as midwives, nurses, dental prosthesis technicians and paramedical health personnel (such as health officers) authorized to practise circumcision.

§1. Authorization to Work as a Physician

96. According to the law, only those persons who have graduated from a faculty of medicine may practice as a physician in Turkey (Article 1), and their diploma must be approved by the Ministry of Health (Article 2). The same article states that diplomas of military physicians must also be approved by the Ministry.

I. Qualifications for Practising as a Medical Doctor in Turkey

97. A medical intervention can only be performed by an authorized person. Apart from exceptional situations, this authority has been delegated to physicians only. Individuals eligible for practising as physicians have been defined in LPOMRA and Turkish Physicians Association Law (*Türk Tabipler Birliği Kanunu*) (TPAL), dating from 1953. The requirements for practising medicine as a physician are listed below.

A. Being a Turkish Citizen

98. Article 1 of LPOMRA states that to work as a physician and administer treatment procedures, the person must be a Turkish citizen. With the amendment of 2 November 2011, the definition of 'Turkish citizens' changed to 'physicians' and 'to have a diploma from Turkish Medical Faculty' is also changed to 'to have a diploma from a medical faculty'.

B. Possessing a Diploma in Medicine

99. The second requirement for practising medicine as a physician is possessing a diploma or degree in medicine, as stated in Article 1. Further, Article 2 states that the diploma must be obtained in Turkey and must be approved by the Ministry of Health. Under certain conditions, diplomas obtained by Turkish citizens in other countries are also valid. According to Article 4 of LPOMRA, the latter type of diploma is to be examined by a commission established by the Ministry of Health.

Several criteria are considered, including the duration of the education and training period and the curriculum of the school granting the diploma. If the diploma was obtained from a school of medicine whose programme length and curriculum were equivalent to those in Turkey, the diploma is considered valid and the graduate is authorized to practise medicine. In contrast, if the diploma has been obtained from a school lacking these qualities, the graduate is required to first complete his/her education, including clinical rotation requirements. The graduate is then required to pass an examination by a board of medical professors. Graduates who successfully pass this examination are granted permission to practise medicine.

C. Registration with the Chamber of Physicians

100. To be eligible for practising medicine as a physician in Turkey, one must be registered with the Chamber of Physicians of the local area. According to Article 7 of TPAL, any physician willing to practise his/her profession within the borders of the region is obliged to register with the Chamber of Physicians. The obligation for physicians working in the public sector to register was a controversial issue before 1983; however, an amendment in 1983 clarified the issue. Accordingly, physicians serving in the public sector are not required to register with the Chamber of Physicians.

D. No Permanent or Temporary Barriers to Practise Medicine

101. Article 28 of LPOMRA includes the list of conditions where an individual is considered permanently banned from practising medicine. Individuals sentenced to imprisonment for more than five years or sanctioned to severe imprisonment regardless of the duration may not work as physicians. Similarly, individuals permanently banned from public service or from the medical profession may not practice medicine. In addition, individuals with documented incurable mental conditions that may impede medical practice may not practice as physicians. However, the banning of individuals from medical practice due to sanctions imposed for criminal offences unrelated to medicine is a controversial issue and is criticized in the legal doctrine.[16]

II. The Authority to Perform Medical Interventions

102. With few exceptions, Turkish law grants the authority to perform medical procedures to physicians who have earned a diploma from a faculty of medicine that is approved by the Ministry of Health, as stated clearly in Article 8. Similarly, the authority to perform dental interventions has been given to dentists, as defined in Article 34.

16. Bayraktar, *supra* para. 32, n. 1, s. 9.

A. *Other Individuals Qualified to Perform a Medical Intervention*

103. Article 3 of LPOMRA states that under certain exceptional conditions, health officers and emergency medical technicians may perform medical interventions. This article, amended in 1993, states that privates and corporals who are serving their compulsory military duty in the Turkish Armed Forces and are recruited to serve as paramedical personnel may perform minor medical interventions. This provision, however, applies only during the time of the fulfilment of their compulsory military service.

B. *The Authority to Perform Surgical Interventions*

104. Article 3 of LPOMRA further states that general practitioners may not perform major surgical interventions, though minor surgical procedures may be performed by all physicians. Article 23 states that major surgical procedures requiring local or general anaesthesia may be performed by general practitioners under the supervision of specialists. According to the same article, health officers who have graduated from schools under the management of the Ministry of Health (or from equally qualified schools), with a diploma approved by the Ministry of Health, may also perform minor surgical interventions. In addition, Article 3 states that health officers possessing the necessary qualifications defined in the law are allowed to perform circumcisions.

C. *Emergency Situations*

105. In situations requiring major surgery, if a specialist is not available immediately or cannot be contacted, the intervention may be performed by a general practitioner. Article 23 states that general practitioners may perform major surgical procedures in extraordinary situations.

With an amendment made in 2005, emergency medical technicians were granted the authority to perform medical interventions, but only in situations of medical emergencies.

D. *Advertisement Ban*

106. Article 24 allows physicians practising medicine to provide advertisements describing the location and time they receive their patients. However, it is prohibited for physicians to provide commercials. This issue was addressed in MDR, Article 8, which states that professionals in medicine, dentistry and healthcare institutions are not to be perceived as commercial entities and must uphold the dignity of their respective professions. Accordingly, they are prohibited from placing advertisements with commercial content in newspapers and other mass media.[17] Article 9 of the Regulation states that the advertisements and prescription forms may only include the medical professional's name, surname, address, speciality, academic title and work hours. Restrictions regarding the signboards on buildings were also defined in Article 9.

E. Criminal Sanctions

107. Individuals using the title of physician or practising medicine without a valid diploma will be imprisoned for terms ranging from six months to six years. However, if a more severe sanction is imposed in the Turkish Penal Code, the Penal Code Sanctions will apply, as stated in Article 25.

Article 26 states that physicians not authorized to practise medicine as defined in this law will be sanctioned with a monetary fine.

17. For a detailed review of this issue with regard to dentistry in Turkish legislations and medical deontology, *see* Ş. Görkey, Dişhekimliği Deontolojisi ve Reklamlar-II *(Dental Deontology and Advertisements-II)* Dergi, İstanbul Dişhekimleri Odası Dergisi, Sayı 24, Aralık 1991, ss 16–18; and P. Kökdemir & Ş. Görkey, Diş Hekimliğinde Reklamın Etik Boyutu ve İnternet Kulanımı *(The Ethical Aspects of Advertising and the Use of Internet in Dentistry).* Türkiye Biyoetik Derneği II. Ulusal Tıbbi Etik Kongresi Bildiri Kitabı. Ed. Arda, B., Akdur, R., Aydın, E. 18–20 Ekim Kapadokya 2001, ss 455–466.

Chapter 3. Control over the Practice of Medicine

§1. Professional Liability

108. Turkish law defines civil, criminal, administrative and disciplinary liabilities for physicians. While specific regulations for the physician's practice do not exist, the liabilities mentioned above are determined within the framework established by the legislation in civil law, obligations law, criminal and administrative law.

Medical procedures performed by authorized persons that provide direct or indirect therapeutic benefits are considered medical interventions. Interventions carried out to prevent or alleviate an abnormality or a deficiency are included within the scope of this definition.

The physician performing the medical procedure must follow the rules defined in the relevant laws and regulations and act in accordance with the contract between him/her and the patient. Acting otherwise will result in criminal and civil liabilities for the physician. Relevant laws and legislation include Law on the Practice of Medicine and Related Arts *(Tababet ve Şuabatı Sanatlarının Tarz-ı İcrasına Dair Kanun)* (LPOMRA), the General Health Law *(Umumi Hıfzıssıhha Yasası)*, TPAL, MDR and the Regulation on Patient Rights *(Hasta Hakları Yönetmeliği)* (RPR).

109. Specialist physicians trained in a surgical branch may perform surgery within the limits of their speciality. Article 3 of LPOMRA states that specialist training is a prerequisite for performing surgical interventions. Apart from medical emergencies where immediate intervention is vital, general practitioners performing surgery are considered to act against their obligation to provide due care. Interns, that is, final (sixth) year students in the faculties of medicine, have been permitted to participate in outpatient clinical activities. Since these students act under the supervision of the university staff members, their activities are not considered an independent medical intervention. In Turkish legal doctrine, it is noted that the practice of interns should be considered in the same context as other healthcare personnel (e.g., nurses and technicians).[18]

I. Civil Liability

110. The civil liability of a physician due to medical interventions performed during independent medical practice may arise in three ways: (1) the liability occurring from the 'contract' between the patient and the physician; (2) tort liability; and (3) liability due to working without mandate which involves interventions based on the patient's presumed consent.[19]

---

18. Ayan, *supra* para. 45, n. 1. s. 97.
19. *Ibid.,* s. 49; S. Reisoğlu, Hekimlerin Hukuki Sorumluluğu Sorumluluk Hukukundaki Yeni Gelişmeler *(Civil Liability of Physicians. New Developments in Liability Law).* V. Sempozyumu İstanbul 1983, s. 3 vd.; Ç. Aşçıoğlu Tıbbi Yardım ve El Atmalardan Doğan Sorumluluklar *(Liabilities Arising from Medical Care and Medical Interventions).* Ankara 1993, s. 64 vd.

A. Liability Arising from the Contract

111. The approach in Turkish law for determining the physician's legal liability is based on the idea of a contract considered to exist between the physician and the patient. Apart from medical emergencies, the physician's intervention is justified on the grounds of this contract, known as the 'treatment contract' or 'physician contract'. This contract imposes duties on physicians such that physicians must provide the necessary services to diagnose the disease and administer the appropriate form of treatment, commensurate with the 'state of the art' in medical science.[20]

1. Characteristics of the Treatment Contract

112. The treatment contract is based on the concepts of 'body integrity' and 'health', which can be harmed in ways that are difficult to recompense. Thus, the due care expected of the physician has higher standards than those in other contracts.

113. Another important aspect of the treatment contract involves the unequal standing of the physician and the patient with regard to the information about the issue of the contract. The physician's superior medical knowledge places the patient in an inferior position relative to the physician. For this reason, the concept of 'trust' emerges as the other essential element of the treatment contract. In addition, this contract does not require the result of the treatment to be guaranteed by the physician. Such a guarantee is difficult to offer because the results of the treatment depend not only on the physician's intervention and capabilities but also on other external factors that may affect the results of the treatment.[21]

2. Status of the Treatment Contract in Civil Law

114. In Turkish legal doctrine, there is a consensus with regard to the scope and the content of the treatment contract established between the patient and the physician during the medical intervention. There are, however, different opinions regarding the legal status of this contract. In Turkish legal doctrine, as in the Swiss legal doctrine, it is generally agreed that a treatment contract is a contract of mandate.[22]

20. Yargıtay 4. Hukuk Dairesi (*Turkish High Court of Appeals, 4. Judicial Law Office*), dated 7 Mar. 1977 verdict No. 2541.
21. C. Yavuz, Borçlar Hukuku Özel Hükümler (*Obligations Law Specific Provisions*) (Istanbul: Beta Basim Yayin, 1996). s. 452.
22. Ayan, *supra* para. 45, n. 1, s. 53; *see also* Yavuz, *supra* para. 72, n. 1, s. 563; Reisoğlu, *supra* para. 69, n. 1, s. 13; S. Donay, Meslek Sırrının Açıklanması Suçu (*The Offence of Disclosing Professional Secret*). İ.Ü. Yayınları Sulhi Goran Matbaası, İstanbul, 1978, s. 46.

115. Certain medical interventions are considered in the scope of the work contract in Turkish legal doctrine,[23] and this approach is also observed in some rulings made by the High Court of Appeals (*Yargıtay*). For example, plastic surgery procedures and crown and bridge prostheses in dentistry are defined within the scope of the work contract. The High Court of Appeals, thirteenth Judicial Law Office, declared in one of its rulings that plastic surgery is compatible with the work contract, where the result of the act (rather than the performance of the act) is paramount and the achieved result should be objectively observable.[24]

In a case ruled by the High Court of Appeals on 20 December 1977,[25] the court declared that the contract involved in the making of a dental prosthesis was a work contract. The ruling stated that 'whether the prosthesis made by the claimant is compatible with the requirements of the work contract, and whether this prosthesis is scientifically and medically suitable for use by the respondent P.S. [post-surgery] and acceptable *ex aequo et bono*, is to be re-examined by an expert, in accordance with the Obligations Law, Article 475, and a verdict is to be reached based upon the expert's report', considering only the materials and technique used in the making of the prosthesis for determining the dentist's liability.

Therefore, Turkish legal doctrine can be considered to view the treatment contract as a form of contract of mandate. The treatment contract involves the patient (client) who is under the obligation to pay the physician (delegate), and the physician who is under a series of obligations to achieve a result that is in accordance with the benefit and will of the patient. The goal of the contract is to ensure that the necessary activities to restore the health of the patient will be carried out in accordance with the patient's demands and benefits. Verdicts by the High Court of Appeals have been declared within this framework.[26,27,28,29]

Thus, the content and the scope of the treatment contract are compatible with the characteristics of the contract of mandate, as stated in the Turkish Obligations Law's Article 502. Accordingly, the physician is not under obligation to guarantee that the result (namely, restoring health) will be achieved. Due to the nature of the treatment contract, the result cannot be guaranteed. In addition, the absence of a time constraint for the performance of the obligation and the performance of the obligation independent of the patient are also characteristics that belong to the contract of mandate.

---

23. Ayan, *supra* para. 45, n. 1, s. 52.
24. Yargıtay 13. Hukuk Dairesi (*Turkish High Court of Appeals, 13th Judicial Law Office*), dated 5 Apr. 1993, verdict No. 2741.
25. Yargıtay 15. Hukuk Dairesi (*Turkish High Court of Appeals, 15th Judicial Law Office*), dated 20 Dec. 1977, verdict No. 2307.
26. Yargıtay 9. Hukuk Dairesi (*Turkish High Court of Appeals, 9th Judicial Law Office*), dated 18 Nov. 1991, verdict No. 8375.
27. Yargıtay 13. Hukuk Dairesi (*Turkish High Court of Appeals, 13th Judicial Law Office*), dated 8 Jul. 2005, verdict No. 11796.
28. Yargıtay Hukuk Genel Kurulu (*High Court of Appeals General Council of Judicial Law*), dated 11 Dec. 2002, verdict No. 1047.
29. H. Savaş, Sağlık Çalışanlarının ve Sağlık Kurumlarının Tıbbi Müdahaleden Doğan Sorumluluklari *(The Liabilities of Health Care Workers and Health Care Institutions in Medical Interventions)* 1 (Ankara: Baskı, Seçkin Yayıncılık, 2007). ss 100–101.

3. Responsibilities of the Physician Regarding the Treatment Contract

116. The treatment contract implies that the physician has undertaken an obligation. As stated above, this obligation requires the physician to provide due care, acting in accordance with the state-of-the-art medical science to restore the patient's health. The physician fulfils the duties of his/her treatment contract by acting professionally and fulfilling his/her medical responsibilities during the intervention involving the patient's care.

117. Treatment, which is the main element of the physician's obligation, can be grouped into two different components: diagnosis and treatment. Several obligations due to Obligations Law and other legislation arise within the context of these two main components.

a. Diagnosis

118. Correct diagnosis of a disease is essential in choosing the appropriate method of treatment. For this reason, all the necessary medical data (such as obtaining medical history, physical examination, laboratory tests, X-rays) should be acquired and a proper diagnosis should be made. If all the required procedures have been performed with due care, the physician will not be responsible for an incorrect diagnosis in terms of the provisions provided in the MDR.

b. Choosing and Performing a Method of Treatment

119. The physician must perform the method that will be most beneficial and least harmful to the patient. MDR's (*Tıbbi Deontoloji Tüzüğü*) Articles 6 and 10 include provisions on this principle. Article 6 states, 'The physician and the dentist act on conscience and by using professional judgment, without any influence and interference.' All the necessary precautions for preventing harm to the patient (such as using sterile equipment) should be taken while the treatment is being performed. Accordingly, the physician taking all the necessary precautions during the performance of the chosen treatment method will not be liable if the treatment is unsuccessful.

Article 10 includes provisions on the use of newly developed or discovered treatment methods. It states that if a treatment modality different than that usually applied is to be recommended, then the physician should be of the opinion that the method will be more beneficial than other methods and will not harm the patient. In addition, the article bans the use of statements about a new discovery that might be misleading.

c. Providing Due Care

120. Physicians are expected to provide due care during the treatment of the patient.

121. Obligations Law, Article 506, includes provisions on the obligation of the delegate (which would correspond to the physician in the case of the treatment contract) to act with due care. When considered in the context of the physician's responsibility, these provisions imply that the physician is responsible for performing the act with due care, rather than obtaining the intended result of the act. Therefore, the physician should perform the required interventions and activities to obtain the intended result and avoid any acts that will prevent the achieving of this goal. The same article states that the due care that should be provided by the representative should be the same due care that should be provided by the worker. The term 'worker' implies the party undertaking the responsibility to carry out a given task.

122. The duty to provide due care by the worker was determined in Article 396 of Obligations Law: any harm caused by intentional, negligent and careless acts will result in liability. The degree of due care required is determined by the importance of the act. Since healthcare procedures involve health, a maximum degree of due care should be provided.

d. The Obligation of the Physician to Personally Intervene

123. Another important duty for the physician is to perform the required act personally. In addition, according to the principles of the contract of mandate, the representative should act in accordance with the client's instructions. Since the treatment contract involves the intervention of an expert, however, the patient (the client) has very limited opportunity to instruct the physician.

e. Obligation of Fidelity

124. During the fulfilment of an obligation, the physician is required to protect the health and safety of his/her patient, in accordance with the trust placed in him/her by the patient. Obligations such as truthful disclosure and medical confidentiality are a result of the physician's obligation of fidelity, which remains in effect after the termination of the contract.

i. Informing the Patient

125. Informing the patient is an essential responsibility of the physician. In addition to provisions on the protection of individual rights and liberties in the Constitution and in the Civil Code, there are also several regulations containing provisions on the duty of the physician to inform a patient prior to a medical intervention. These regulations include LPOMRA (Article 70), MDR (Article 14) and Law on Procurement, Storage and Grafting of Tissues and Organs (*Organ ve Doku Alınması, Saklanması, Aşılanması ve Nakli Hakkında Kanun*) (LOT) (Article 7).

ii. The Obligation to Protect the Interests of the Patient

126. Another duty considered to arise from the obligation of fidelity is the physician's obligation to uphold the interests of the patient over his/her own. The treatment contract between the physician and the patient involves the body integrity and health of the individual, which are superior to individual values. For this reason, in cases where the physician's and patient's interests conflict, the physician should be able to forfeit his/her own interests in order to fulfil his/her duty of fidelity.

iii. Professional Confidentiality

127. The physician is obliged to protect the confidential information he/she has learned throughout the treatment process. While Obligations Law contains no clear provision on the obligation to maintain confidentiality, this duty arises as a result of the obligations of trust and fidelity. In addition, the duty to maintain confidentiality is an obligation arising from public law, particularly for certain professionals such as physicians and lawyers who carry out certain tasks within the context of their profession, as stated in Articles 134 and 137 of the Turkish Penal Code. Further, Article 4 of MDR prohibits physicians from divulging secrets learned during the practice of their profession.

4. Liability of the Physician Arising from the Activities of Paramedical Personnel

128. It is customary for physicians to use paramedical personnel. However, according to Obligations Law, Article 506, the representative must personally fulfil the required task within the contract of mandate scheme due to the importance of trust placed in him/her as a representative. Conversely, it is not realistic to expect all the activities within the scope of treatment contract to be performed by the physician himself/herself. The physician may use paramedical personnel or may transfer his/her obligation to a third person. Activities such as injections, preparing the patient for surgery and sterilization of equipment are among the obligations that can be transferred to a third person. People who perform such obligations are paramedical personnel and healthcare workers, including nurses, laboratory and X-ray technicians. Under certain circumstances, dental prosthesis technicians may also be considered as paramedical personnel within this context.

Physicians are liable for the harm that might be caused by paramedical personnel's actions, as stated in Obligations Law, Article 116.[30] Accordingly, it is not adequate for the physician to disclaim liability by proving that he/she acted with due care during the selection and instruction of paramedical personnel.

Further, if the paramedical personnel's act constitutes tort, the patient may sue his/her physician even when the physician has no fault, based on Article 66 of Obligations Law. However, for the physician to be liable for a tort committed by his/her paramedical personnel, an employment relationship must be present between the

30. Ayan, *supra* para. 45, n. 1, ss 68–69; S. Tekinay, et al., Tekinay, Borçlar Hukuku Genel Hükümler (*Obligations Law General Provisions*) 7 (İstanbul Baskı Filiz Kitabevi 1993), s. 899.

physician and the personnel. It is generally accepted that such a relationship exists between physicians and nurses or official caregivers. The physician will also be liable if the harm occurred during the fulfilment of the service and in relation to the service. The activities of nurses and caregivers usually involve such service.

B. Tort Liability of the Physician

1. Tort

129. Since a contract is considered to exist between the patient and the physician in Turkish law, the liability of the physician is determined in accordance with the provisions of the contract of mandate. However, the physician might also be subject to tort liability.

130. Any harm caused by the physician to the physical integrity of the patient could be considered as tort according to Obligations Law, Article 49. However, for the physician to be liable due to the provisions of Article 49, the elements of unlawfulness, fault, damage and link of causation should be present.

2. Unlawfulness

131. Unlawfulness implies that the legal norm, which prohibits direct or indirect damage to others, has been violated. An unlawful act contains behaviour against the laws that aim to protect the values of individuals and their personal property.

Unlawfulness in tort liability is equivalent to violating a contract in the contractual responsibility. According to the Turkish Obligations Law, the physician may be subject to tort liability regardless of the existence of a contract. However, if the physician inflicts damage in violation of the contract, or if the physician fails to act in accordance with the obligations imposed upon him/her with the contract, he/she may be subject to both tort liability and liability arising from the contract. Therefore, the patient may sue the physician on the basis of any of these two legal grounds. There are differences with regard to the legal procedures involved in these two claims. In lawsuits filed on the grounds of violation of contract, the burden of proof belongs to the physician, whereas in tort liability, the burden of proof belongs to the patient. Lawsuits alleging the violation of the contract should be filed within one year of the plaintiff becoming aware of the damage and within no more than five years. The time limit in tort liability cases is ten years. Turkish legal doctrine suggests that the patient may follow either option, tort liability or contract violation, depending on the subjective conditions of the individual.[31]

If the medical intervention has been carried out in accordance with the current standards of medical science and practice and on lawful grounds, then the physician may not be subject to tort liability. Thus, obtaining a blood sample from a driver for

31. Ayan. Tıbbi Müdahalelerden Doğan Sorumluluk (*Civil Liability Arising From the Medical Intervention*) (Ankara: Kazancı Hukuk Yayınları, 1991), ss 116–117.

blood alcohol level examination without obtaining his/her prior consent will not constitute tort, but only if the physician had been requested by the police to obtain the sample.[32]

In Turkish law, unlawfulness must be proven by the patient.

3. Fault

132. The second requirement for establishing tort liability is the fault component. To establish fault, the physician must have acted knowingly or must have desired the unlawful consequence. In addition, the physician must have failed to provide due care which normally would be provided by a conventional physician acting under the same conditions. The burden of proof for fault belongs to the patient in tort liability.

4. Damage

133. In order to be liable in tort, the unlawful act of the physician must cause damage. If no damage has occurred as a result of the act of the physician, then the physician will not be liable for tort even when fault is involved. If damage has occurred as a result of the physician's fault, then physical and moral indemnity may be demanded. Damage in tort liability must be proven by the patient.

5. Link of Causation

134. The damage inflicted upon the patient must be caused by the unlawful act of the physician. If there is no link of causation between the damage and the act, or, if the link has been severed due to the patient's fault, then the physician will not be subject to tort liability. The burden of establishing the link of causation between the physician's act and the inflicted damage belongs to the patient. On 30 January 2010, supplement article to LPOMRA, physicians should make compulsory insurance for their malpractice possibilities. This article includes all physicians and dentists who work in state or private healthcare institutions or private practice.

II. Criminal Liability

A. Introduction

135. A physician acts to prevent and treat disorders or ameliorate the clinical course of a disease. Such acts may result in success or, sometimes, in failure.

32. In all other conditions involving physical examination, a judge's order or a court order – and in emergency cases, a prosecutor's order – is necessary. This issue was addressed in Art. 75 of Law on Penal Trials issued in 2004.

Therefore, a medical intervention may cause deterioration of the individual's health, or may even cause death. Such acts comply with intentional murder or negligent murder and battery and require criminal sanction. The physician's criminal liability is established within the framework set out by the general provisions of the Turkish Penal Code.

B. Historical Background

136. Until the *Tanzimat* era (a reformation period of the Ottoman Empire in the nineteenth century), the legal status of physicians was regulated by the orders of the Ottoman crown (*ferman*) and the instructions of the head physicians (*hekimbası*). Some court judgments also include information about the practice of physicians. In two court judgments from the Ottoman period, it is understood that the physician was judged liable for not obtaining his/her patient's consent to treatment.[33] This indicates that heretofore the consent of the patient had not been considered a requirement for the lawfulness of the treatment. In addition, there are orders of the crown addressing the training and activities of physicians. For instance, in an order by Sultan Mustafa III (1717–1774), practising medicine without a licence was prohibited and was declared that such practice would be punished.[34]

Starting from the *Tanzimat* era, activities related to healthcare were addressed within the scope of written laws. The Penal Code enacted in 1858 included more comprehensive provisions with regard to the criminal liability of the physicians. In Articles 192 and 193, the criminal sanctions for procuring an abortion were increased. Article 215 of the same Code defines the disclosure of confidential patient information as a criminal offence. In addition, Article 182 addresses negligent murder. Following the legal doctrine of the time, it was declared that these provisions would apply when an individual died as a result of a physician's incompetence, unskilful intervention or clear mistake.[35]

C. Criminal Liability in Turkish Law

137. There are different views in the Turkish legal doctrine with regard to the criminal liability of the physician and whether physicians' activities should be considered within the scope of the criminal offences defined in the law. The dominant view on the issue asserts that physicians' activities will not constitute a criminal offence since the aspect of unlawfulness is not present.[36]

Since training and education on medical interventions are legally allowed and regulated by the relevant health legislation, interventions in this field are considered

33. Bayraktar, *supra* para. 32, n. 1, s. 61.
34. A.H. Bayat, Şeriye Sicilleri ve Tıp Tarihimiz I Rıza Senetleri (*Ottoman Court Records and Our Medical History I Consent Forms*) (Ankara, Türk Tarih Kurumu Basımevi, 1999), ss 40–41; K. Bayraktar, *supra* para. 32, n. 1, ss 61–62.
35. Bayraktar, *supra* para. 32, n. 1, ss 61–62; A.H. Bayat, *supra* ss 40–41.
36. Bayraktar, *supra* para. 32, n. 1, ss 105–106.

lawful. The right to perform a medical intervention has been recognized primarily for physicians. For instance, Article 1 of MDR states that physicians may perform activities for diagnostic and therapeutic purposes that are based on scientific evidence of necessity.

In addition, physicians perform their activities to carry out the obligations imposed on them by certain laws. Certain interventions in the field of public health are based on legal duties imposed on physicians. For instance, General Health Law (*Umumi Hıfzıssıhha Yasası*), issued in 1930, imposes compulsory medical treatment for some communicable diseases. In a similar vein, the obligation of the physician to intervene in medical emergencies has been addressed in MDR, Article 3.

However, aside from the conditions in the law detailed above, informed consent of the individual is essential for justifying the lawfulness of a medical intervention (LPOMRA, Article 70). This means that medical interventions performed by an authorized physician on an individual without the consent of that person cannot be considered lawful, unless the intervention is compatible with the exceptions addressed in the law. In addition, informed consent plays a key role in defining the limits of medical intervention.

Lawful medical interventions will not be subject to criminal liability. For medical interventions, the physician's legal authorization to practise medicine, his/her obtaining the consent of the individual and performing the interventions within the limits of medical science are the essential elements of lawfulness.[37]

1. Legal Authorization to Practise Medicine

138. For the situation in Turkish law, *see* paragraphs 97–101.

2. Obtaining the Consent of the Individual

139. The consent of the individual is an important aspect in Turkish law for justifying the lawfulness of a medical intervention, as well as for defining the limits of the intervention. A valid consent given with free will by the patient requires disclosure. The information to be disclosed must include the scope of the intervention, probable consequences, risks, side effects and alternative treatment methods available. If the obligation to inform the patient is not fulfilled, then the medical intervention may become unlawful, and the physician may be subject to criminal liability in such cases.

140. Article 26 of RPR states that the consent of the individual should be obtained before the intervention or during the time of the intervention. Accordingly, if the patient is younger than 18 years of age or incompetent to decide, the permission of the parent/legal representative should be obtained. Although not clearly

37. H. Hakeri, Tıp Hukuku (*Medical Law*). Seçkin Yayıncılık San. Tic. A.Ş. Ankara, 2007, ss 286–287.

defined in the text, the Regulation here seems to make a distinction between 'consent' and 'permission', with consent corresponding to the favourable decision of the competent individual, whereas permission implies the favourable decision made by the parent/legal representative. In addition, the Regulation states that the minor should be included in the decision-making process as much as possible. However, no age limit has been determined for this procedure.

141. However, a physician may intervene on the basis of presumed consent under certain conditions, such as when the patient is unconscious. Further, in some situations, seeking the consent of the individual may give rise to medical drawbacks. For instance, extending or changing the scope of a medical intervention that has already been initiated (i.e., during a surgical intervention performed under general anaesthesia) may be done on the basis of presumed consent. Such situations will not constitute unlawfulness. However, Turkish legal doctrine[38] requires that such exceptions be limited to situations where seeking the consent of the individual or his/her proxy would be life-threatening.

3. Physician Liability Arising from Unlawful Acts

142. Medical interventions aim to protect the life, health and body integrity of persons. However, medical interventions may also endanger such valuable assets while trying to protect them at the same time. This means that, regardless of the goal of the intervention, the interventional act may violate certain fundamental rights, such as a patient's right to health and bodily integrity. Unless the element of lawfulness is present, the physician will be liable.

The consent of the individual prior to treatment, intervention by a legally authorized person to practise medicine and intervening within limits defined by the art and science of medicine constitute the main elements of lawfulness for questioning the legal status of a medical intervention. In addition, the presence of fault may also render the act unlawful.

143. When interventions directed towards the physical integrity of individuals result in injury, such conditions may imply criminal liability due to negligent assault or negligent murder. For instance, a dentist was convicted of assault for removing the wrong tooth of his/her patient by a verdict of the High Court of Appeals.[39] In another case, a lawsuit was filed following the death of a traffic accident victim who had been brought to the hospital for treatment. It was decided by the High Court of Appeals that the physician and nurse could be liable for the death of the patient due to their failure to take the necessary precautions to prevent such a result.[40,41]

---

38. Ayan, *supra* para. 45, n. 1, ss 68–69; Tekinay, et al., *supra* para. 87, n. 1, s. 80.
39. Yargıtay 4. Ceza Dairesi (*High Court of Appeals, 4th Penal Office*), dated 12 Nov. 2003, verdict No. 11352.
40. Savaş, *supra* para. 74, n. 7, ss 286–287.
41. Yargıtay 4. Ceza Dairesi (*High Court of Appeals, 4th Penal Office*), dated 11 Feb. 2004, verdict No. 2055.

144. Additional criminal liability may arise due to other criminal offences addressed in the Turkish Penal Code, or based on certain provisions in legislation regulating the practice of medicine, as outlined in the last paragraph of this section.

4. Liability Arising from Intentional Unlawful Acts (Unlawful Conduct Motivated by Premeditated or Intentional Purposes)

145. Criminal liability of a physician for an intentional unlawful act (unlawful conduct motivated by a premeditated or intentional purpose) is a rarely encountered situation.[42] To be subject to such liability, the physician is required to have acted on the knowledge and desire of the harmful outcome, as stated in Article 21 of the Turkish Penal Code, 2005.[43]

To be charged with intentional murder, a physician must have acted on the knowledge and desire that death would result as the consequence of the act. The legal status of active euthanasia may be evaluated within this framework. Turkish law does not contain a specific regulation for active euthanasia, and the act of active euthanasia is considered an intentional murder. In addition, the RPR clearly forbids euthanasia. It is defended in Turkish legal doctrine that, under certain conditions, active euthanasia should be addressed in the Penal Code as a specific criminal offence that requires less severe sanctions than intentional murder.[44] However, no changes were made regarding this issue in the recent Turkish Penal Code issued in 2005. Thus, the legal status of active euthanasia has remained unchanged in Turkish law and is considered intentional murder.

5. Negligence Liability

146. Avoiding negligence is of particular importance in medical interventions. Criminal liability due to negligence is addressed in Article 22 of the Turkish Penal Code. Negligence liability arises when due diligence and care have not been provided during medical interventions.

However, not all harmful consequences will imply negligence. Medical interventions inhere certain risks and possible complications. A complication arising within the defined limits of the art and science of medicine will not give rise to criminal liability. Further, situations where no precaution can be taken to prevent a harmful outcome or where a harmful outcome occurs despite the precautions taken will not constitute criminal liability for the physician. It is important to assess the foreseeable and unforeseeable risks that may result where no precautions are or can be taken. For instance, in a lawsuit filed against a dentist due to lesions occurring on

42. K. İçel, Hekimin Hukuksal Sorumluluğu (*The Legal Responsibility of the Doctor*). Türkiye Biyoetik Derneği Uluslararası Katılımlı 3. Ulusal Tıp Etiği Kongresi Kongre Kitabı. Ed.: Erdemir, A.D., Uzel, İ, Öncel, Ö., Oğuz, Y., Aksoy, Ş., Şahinoğlu, S., Kadıoğlu, S., Büken, N.Ö., Doğan, H., Yetener, M., Atıcı, E.C. 1. Bursa, 2003, s. 26.
43. Bayraktar, *supra* para. 32, n. 1, s. 203.
44. S. Inceoğlu, Ötanazi. Ölme hakkı (*Euthanasia. The Right to Die*). Ayrıntı Yayınları, İstanbul, 1999, ss 75–76.

the patient's face following radiotherapy, the expert report determined that the consequence was due to the sensitivity of the patient and found no fault on the part of the dentist. However, the High Court of Appeals decided that performing such a procedure without investigating the sensitivity of the patient to such a procedure was negligent and thus considered the act of the dentist as negligence.[45,46]

It may be concluded that a physician's negligent act resulting in harm to the patient will require criminal sanctions for negligent battery or negligent murder, depending on the outcome of the act.

6. Other Forms of Criminal Liability Relevant to Medical Practice

147. In addition to intentional or negligent battery or murder, criminal liability may arise for physicians due to certain interventions performed in their medical practice. Several examples of such acts have been addressed in the Penal Code. When not performed in accordance with the relevant legal framework, experimentation on humans (Article 90), tissue or organ removal (Article 91), abortion (Article 99) and sterilization procedures (Article 101) may be considered within this context. Unlawful disclosure of personal data (Articles 136, 137) and invasion of personal privacy (Article 134) are also evaluated within this scheme.

148. Furthermore, criminal offences have been defined in various legislations that regulate the practice of medicine. Article 70 of LPOMRA defines medical intervention performed without consent as wrongdoing. If such intervention resulted in bodily harm or death, then such an act would also be evaluated within the relevant provisions of the Penal Code discussed above. Additionally, Article 26 of the LPOMRA defines unauthorized medical practice as a wrongful act requiring sanction.

III. Investigations Against Healthcare Personnel

149. In line with the amendment made in the Fundamental Law on Health Care Services with the Law No. 7406, beginning the investigations against healthcare personnel is dependent on the permission of the Professional Responsibility Board established under the Ministry of Health. According to additional Article 18 of the law, physicians, dentists and other healthcare professionals working in public or private healthcare institutions and organizations and foundation universities are subject to the regulation. Practices subject to the investigation cover medical practices related to the examination, diagnosis and treatment performed by the aforementioned health personnel. Decisions of the Professional Responsibility Board can be appealed. Detailed provisions are included in the regulation dated 15 June 2022. The

---

45. Savaş, *supra* para. 74, n. 7, s. 151.
46. Yargıtay 4. Hukuk Dairesi (*High Court of Appeals, 4th Judiciary Office*) dated 12 Dec. 1976, verdict No. 11046.

Professional Responsibility Board is also authorized to decide on the responsibilities of physicians, dentists and other healthcare professionals who are determined to have intentionally abused their public duties based on the finalized criminal court decision. The Professional Responsibility Board determines whether the compensation paid by the administration can be claimed from the relevant healthcare personnel due to the medical practice of the person concerned and the amount of the claim. Physicians, dentists and other healthcare professionals working in public institutions and organizations and state universities are subject to this provision.

150. The Board should be established by the Deputy Minister (as chairman of the board); General Managers or Assistants of Health Services, Public Hospitals, Legal Services, Management Services; It should consist of seven members, one of whom is a professor or an associate professor. One of the two physicians should be from the internal medicine and the other from one of the surgical branches. The term of the physician members in this committee is two years. Members whose term has expired can be re-elected to the board again. There is no information about the term of office of the other members. The Board should meet at least once a month with the participation of at least four members. Specialized commissions consisting of at least three people can be established to act as advisors and to present their opinions and suggestions on technical and specialist issues to be discussed at the Board meetings. The members of the specialization commission are selected by the President from among the candidates who are experts in the subject proposed by the General Directorate of Health Services. The Minister of Health may create new committees from persons with the same qualifications, under the chairmanship of another Deputy Minister, depending on the nature and agenda of the work.

§2. Disciplinary Organizations

I. The Turkish Physicians Association

151. The TPA was founded on the basis of the TPAL. TPA's aims include protecting the deontological and professional solidarity, ensuring that physicians' efforts are directed towards the benefit of individuals and the public and protecting the rights of the members of the profession. Taking initiatives in the field of public health is also among the goals of the association.

A. Chamber of Physicians

152. TPAL states that a Chamber of Physicians can be established in any city with 200 physicians. In cities with less than 200 physicians, the physicians will be registered with a Chamber of Physicians in another city, depending on the TPA's decision.

1. Becoming a Member of the Chamber of Physicians

153. Physicians in private practice must be registered in the Chamber of Physicians of their local province. Physicians serving in a public healthcare institution may choose to be registered in the Chamber.

2. General Board of the Chamber of Physicians

154. The General Board of the Chamber of Physicians consists of all members of the Chamber. The General Board has several responsibilities, including the review of the annual report on the administrative processes of the Chamber, review and approval of the annual budget and electing the members of the Board of the Chamber of Physicians.

3. The Executive Board of the Chamber of Physicians

155. Members of the Executive Board are elected by the General Board. The Executive Board is responsible for preparing the budget and balance sheet of the Chamber and presenting them to the General Board along with the relevant reports.

a. Duties of the Executive Board of Chamber of Physicians

156. The Executive Board is primarily responsible for ensuring that the medical profession is conducted in accordance with the relevant laws and regulations. Prevention of illegal relations between colleagues, use of intermediaries for finding patients and commercial advertisements are among the board's other responsibilities.

b. Conflicts Between the Colleagues

157. The Executive Board has been assigned the duty to resolve the conflicts occurring between the member physicians of the Chamber in accordance with medical deontology rules.

c. Conflicts Between the Colleagues and the Employers of Physicians

158. The Executive Board may contribute to the negotiation efforts when conflicts arise between colleagues and their employers and may also refer the case to a referee.

d. Conflicts Between the Patients and the Colleagues

159. According to TPAL, the Executive Board resolves patient–member physician conflicts by way of negotiation, considering the dignity of the profession, the severity of the disease and the effort needed to provide healthcare service. Alternatively, the Executive Board may assign a referee to decide on the matter.

160. Further, TPAL assigns significant responsibilities to the Disciplinary Board (DB) of the Chamber and the Higher Disciplinary Board (HDB) of TPA in determining and imposing disciplinary sanctions.

II. The DB of the Chamber of Physicians and the HDB of the TPA

161. TPAL necessitates the formation of DB in each Chamber of Physicians. The members of this board are elected among the members of the General Board; members to be elected to the DB are required to have practised medicine as a physician for a minimum of ten years. In case no such members are present, a minimum of five years of medical practice is sought.

A DB member may be refused participation in a disciplinary hearing if his/her objectivity is in doubt. If such a refusal is justified, then the particular member removes himself/herself from the particular session. In addition, when a DB member is associated with the subject under discussion at a particular DB session, or when the issue concerns the relatives or close acquaintances of a DB member, then that member may not participate in the session.

The DB is authorized to impose penalties upon members who do not fulfil the obligations required by law. Such penalties may consist of a fine, warning and suspension from medical practice for fifteen days to six months. Furthermore, a physician suspended from practice for three times in the same area of jurisdiction may be permanently banned from medical practice.

The disciplinary penalties are announced to the member involved. The member may appeal the decision within fifteen days; otherwise, the decision is final and must be fulfilled. Penalties of temporary suspension must be approved by the HDB of TPA.

162. The HDB consists of nine full-time and nine substitute members who are elected for a period of two years. Each HDB member is required to have a minimum of fifteen years' experience as a practising physician. HDB meetings are held twice per year. The central council or the chair of the last session may convene more frequent meetings if necessary.

Verdicts of the HDB are submitted to the DB of the relevant Chamber of Physicians. The final verdicts are effected by the Ministry of Health.

The HDB reviews the decision reached by a DB. If the HDB does not agree with the DB's opinion, it notifies the relevant DB. If the DB, nonetheless, confirms its initial decision, the case may be reviewed by the HDB for the second time. If the conflict continues, the case then may be taken to the Turkish Council of State (also called Supreme Administrative Court or Danıştay), which is the highest court for resolving administrative conflicts.

III. The Professional Code of Ethics of the TPA

163. The TPA issued its Professional Code of Ethics on 1 February 1999. The Code was accepted at the forty-seventh Congress of TPA, held on 10–11 October 1998.

A. Aim and Scope

164. The rules in the Professional Code of Ethics determine 'the rules of conduct that must be followed by physicians while practicing their profession', as stated in Article 1 of the Code. The rules apply to 'all physicians who are entitled to practice medicine in Turkey'. Article 6 of the Code addresses ethical principles that must be followed while practising medicine. These ethical principles include beneficence, non-maleficence, justice and autonomy.

B. The Duties of the Physician

165. Article 5 of the Code addresses the duties of the physicians, wherein:

> the primary duty of the physician is to protect human health and life by trying to prevent disease and to treat patients, which can be accomplished by fulfilling the requirements of medical science. It is also a primary duty for the physician to respect human dignity during the practice of medicine.

Article 8 emphasizes that the physician is to act in accordance with his/her scientific opinion and by the guidance of his/her personal conscience. Article 12 states that the physician must consider the scientific and contemporary methods of diagnosis and treatment and the essentials of preventive medicine while providing healthcare, and he/she may not resort to non-scientific methods of diagnosis and treatment.

C. Confidentiality

166. Article 9 of the Code addresses confidentiality. Physicians may not disclose confidences they have learned from or about their patients during the practice of their profession. The death of a patient or termination of a patient–physician relationship does not abolish this provision. This article further states that with the consent of the patient, or in cases where maintaining the confidentiality of the information will endanger the life of the patient or others, information may be disclosed if that patient's personal rights are not harmed. In addition, the physician may disclose confidential information when required to do so by law.

167. The physician may refuse to testify as a witness or as an expert in a court when disclosure of confidential information is involved.

D. Emergency Intervention

168. Article 10 of the Code states that physicians, regardless of their duty or speciality, are to intervene in emergency situations where the required medical care cannot otherwise be provided. Article 18 adds that the physician, under situations of medical necessity where a delay in the delivery of healthcare may endanger the patient's life, may perform certain interventions which normally require special training and knowledge.

E. Advertisement Ban

169. Article 11 states that physicians may not advertise while practising medicine, nor may they participate in broadcast commercials or provide their work as a commercial product. Physicians are also prohibited from engaging in behaviour which could mislead or panic people, nor may they cause unjust competition between colleagues.

F. Ban on Relationship for Financial Benefit

170. As stated in Article 14, the physician may not refer his/her patients to other physicians or diagnostic and therapeutic institutions in return for a financial interest. Article 15 forbids physicians from forming any sort of relationship for financial benefit with industrial organizations.

G. Relationships with Other Colleagues (Physician–Physician Relationships)

171. Relationships of a physician with other physicians have also been addressed in the Code. Articles 16 and 17 affirm that the physician must maintain his/her relationships with other physicians in accordance with the relevant principles of the profession. Accordingly, the physician may not display any behaviour that violates the dignity of his/her colleagues. In addition, Article 19 includes rules on consultation and cooperation between physicians from different branches.

H. Patient Rights

172. Several articles include rules on patient rights. Several rights, including the patient's right to be informed (Article 21), the right to informed consent (Article 26), the right to accept or refuse the treatment, the right to choose a physician (Article 22), the right not to know or not to be informed (Article 27) and the right to receive information about himself/herself, have been addressed. Thus, physicians must respect patient rights and fulfil the rules in the RPR.

I. Withdrawal of the Physician from the Therapeutic Relationship

173. Article 25 states that a physician may choose not to undertake the therapeutic responsibility for a patient or may choose to withdraw from the relationship only under conditions where the physician decides that he/she will not be able to use professional medical knowledge as required for the particular patient, and on condition that there is another physician whom the patient may consult. Under such conditions, the physician informs the patient and the relatives that the patient's health will not be placed at risk and gives them information about other physicians available for medical care. The physician may not desert his/her patient until the other physician assumes responsibility. The sending doctor is obligated to transfer all the information of the patient to the receiving doctor.

J. Terminally Ill Patients

174. Article 28 includes provisions declaring that terminally ill patients should be provided with all sorts of humane care, under conditions compatible with human dignity, and that their suffering should be relieved as much as possible.

K. The Obligation to Follow the Provisions of International Conventions

175. The obligation to follow the provisions of international conventions has been emphasized in the Professional Code of Ethics. Article 33 emphasizes the obligation of the physicians to obey all international documents on human rights, including the Universal Declaration of Human Rights and other common rules relevant to medical practice. In addition, Article 34 emphasizes that the physician may not engage in torture and may not prepare any report aiming to conceal such practice. Article 37 bans physicians from taking part in the process of capital punishment.[47]

L. Medical Care for Individuals under Arrest and for Prisoners

176. Prisoners and individuals under arrest, who require medical care, are entitled to all rights recognized for other patients without discrimination (Article 35). In case of treatment refusal, the physician is required to inform such persons about the possible consequences of the refusal. The physician may not resort to compulsory physical examination and treatment (Article 36).

---

47. Capital punishment was abolished in Turkey in 2004.

M. Extraordinary and War Conditions

177. The physician must apply 'The Universal Principles of Ethics under Extraordinary Conditions and in War' in an objective manner. In situations where everyone cannot be provided with the required medical care due to the high number of sick and wounded persons, the physician shall give priority to severe cases that have a high probability of recovery (Article 36).

N. Physical Examination for the Purpose of Detecting Previous Sexual Intercourse

178. Physicians may not perform such physical examination unless ordered to do so by a court or by the directive of a prosecutor. The informed consent of the individual (or the permission of the legal representative if the individual is a minor) must be sought; such examination may not be performed without the individual's consent (Article 37).[48]

O. Research on Human Subjects

179. The rules in the Code regarding research on human subjects have been determined in line with relevant legal regulations in Articles 40, 41, 42 and 43 (*see also*: Experiments on Human Subjects, Part II, Chapter 3, §5).

P. Situations with No Corresponding Provision in the Codes

180. Article 45 deals with cases of a conflict unaddressed by these codes. In such circumstances, the physician is to follow the general principles of ethics and the provisions listed in the relevant national regulations, as well as those in international declarations and conventions.

Q. Disciplinary Prosecution

181. When physicians act against the rules defined in this Code, they are to be referred by the relevant Chamber of Physicians to the appropriate honour board for disciplinary proceedings, in accordance with TPA Law No. 6023. Such disciplinary proceedings are independent of civil or criminal law proceedings. The physician may also be subject to such prosecution in a court of law. The rules of the Code are binding for physicians only.

48. Article 286 of the new Turkish Penal Code (2004) states that such examination may not be performed without the permission of a judge and a prosecutor.

IV. Medical Ethics Committees

A. Historical Background and Recent Developments

182. The need for ethics committees reviewing biomedical research and the lack of specific legislation regulating such research were recognized following an event known as the 'Zakkum Case' in Turkey.[49] A Turkish physician named Ziya Özel claimed to have discovered an anticancer drug which he had developed from *Nerium oleander* (*zakkum*) extract and acquired the patent for the extract. The news stirred public interest, but it was met with considerable scepticism from the academic field. The academics reminded the public that holding a patent does not guarantee the effectiveness of a drug molecule still under development. Özel's claims had no objective scientific basis at the time, lacking clinical evidence obtained from controlled trials, which is the scientific standard required for newly developed drug molecules. In addition to scientific objections, ethical and legal concerns arose as well. All of these concerns need to be addressed within a consistent and objective framework.

The *Zakkum* case and the events following it triggered a response from governmental authorities. Consequently, the Regulation on Drug Trials (RDT) was issued in 1993. This regulation, in addition to being the first specific legislation on clinical drug research in Turkey, also formed the legal basis for the 'Local (Research) Ethics Committees' (LECs) and the 'Central Ethics Committee' (CEC).[50] Ethical review and approval processes of drug trials were carried out in accordance with RDT requirements until 2008. However, the five-year period between 2008 and 2013 was rather problematic; a number of regulations (most recently in 2011) were issued by the Ministry in that period, but some of them were cancelled by the Supreme Administrative Court, causing a rather a chaotic environment with regard to the ethical review of biomedical research on human beings.

---

49. Ş. Görkey, *Research Ethics in Turkey – 12 Years' Experience*. The Regulation and Organization of Research Ethics Review. Report of a Comparative International Workshop held at the Faculty of Law, University of Toronto, 16–18 Jun. 2005 by A. Long, A.S. Kontic, E.C. Barroso, and D. Brinza. Toronto, Canada: Brown Book Company Ltd, 2006, pp. 19–21. For a more detailed review of the history of medical research review processes in Turkey, *see* Ş. Görkey, Ethics Committees and Research in Turkey: Perspectives of Committee Members, Researchers and Industrialists L'Ethique en Mouvement (Ed. C. Herve) Les enjeux de responsabilite poses par les Nouvelles Technologies pour la Sante Publique. Les dossiers d'Ethique Medicale Vol. 1/98 pp. 137–142a; Ş. Görkey, Etik Komiteler (*Ethics Committees*). Sendrom. Şubat 1994: 84–87.
50. For a critical review of the current framework of ethics committees in Turkey and recommendations for improving their function, *see* Ş. Görkey, Avrupa Birliği Üyeliği Sürecinde Türkiye'de Tıp Etiği Alanında Yapılması Gerekenler ve 'Ulusal Etik Komite' Kurulmasının Gerekliliği (*Things to Be Done in the Field of Medical Ethics with Regard to the Turkey's European Union Membership Negotiations Process and the Necessity of Establishing a National Ethics Committee*). II. Ulusal Tıbbi Etik Kongresi Bildiri Kitabı. Editörler: B. Arda, R. Akdur, E. Aydın, 18–20 Ekim 2001. Kapadokya, ss 275–288.

Finally, a new regulation that superseded the 2011 regulation was issued in April 2013. The new regulation is called 'Regulation on Clinical Trials' (*Klinik Araştırmalar Hakkında Yönetmelik*) (RCT), like its predecessors. As the name implies, the new regulation (RCT) has a broader scope and aims to regulate not only drug trials but also other kinds of clinical research.

In addition to citing certain provisions from Turkey's local legislation (additional Article 10 of Law No. 3359; Fundamental Law on Health Care Services and Articles No. 27 and No. 40 of the decree with power of law) for its justification, RCT also cites European Union's directives 2001/20/EC and 2005/28/EC on Good Clinical Practice (GCP).

The local legislation cited in RCT is significant since the decision of the Supreme Administrative Court to cancel one of the previous regulations was justified on the grounds that the Ministry of Health needed to be authorized by a separate law enacted by the Parliament in order to be able to regulate clinical research. However, apparently, the additional article of Law No. 3359 noted above was deemed sufficient for this purpose and no separate law was enacted on the issue.

The new RCT contains thirty-seven articles classified under eight sections. Noteworthy in the first section is Article 2, which explicitly states that retrospective studies are out of the scope of the Regulation, and Article 4, which explains in detail the basic terms and definitions (such as adverse event, bioavailability, clinical drug trial, clinical non-drug research, informed consent, observational drug research, contract research organization) used throughout the Regulation.

The second section at RCT includes Articles 5–8. Article 5 addresses the general ethical principles for human research and strictly forbids any research that aims to alter the genetic structure of the germ cells of volunteers. Articles 6, 7, 8 and 9 address ethical and legal requirements for research on children, pregnant and lactating women, incompetent individuals and intensive care patients/unconscious individuals, respectively. It should be noted that RCT does not categorically forbid research on any of these vulnerable groups; however, a number of requirements need to be fulfilled before clinical research can be conducted on any of these populations (*see also* paragraphs 377–378).

The third section defines the essentials of conducting research procedures (including the requirements for initiating and terminating research) and defines the standards for clinical research locations, whereas sections four and five address respectively the standards for clinical research products and the notification requirements of adverse reactions (including the requirements for confidentiality of records, auditing procedures and administrative sanctions).

B. Central Ethics Committees

183. The RCT detailed above (*see* paragraph 182) does not define a CEC that oversees clinical research, which implies that decision-making authority is granted to the local structures. This is in stark contrast with the 1993 regulation, which clearly favoured a centralized approach on the issue. That being said, Local Research Ethics Committees (LRECs) have to be approved by the Ministry of Health.

184. However, the seventh section of the new RCT now defines a central structure called 'Clinical Research Consultation Board' (CRCB). According to Article 29, this board is to be chaired by a senior bureaucrat from the Ministry of Health and consists of three specialists from each division of medicine (basic sciences, internal medicine and surgical medicine) selected by the Ministry, a psychologist, a theologian and a legal consultant employed or selected by the Ministry. Interestingly, an ethicist is not present among the members of this structure. Article 30 defines the duties of CRCB, which is stated as 'providing expert opinion on issues consulted to the board by either LRECs or researchers'. However, the same article also states that the board takes its decisions with a majority vote. Therefore, although not explicitly stated in the text, it appears that CRCB has been designed to act as the final decision-making authority on the consulted issues.

C. Local (Research) Ethics Committees

185. The sixth section of RCT is entirely devoted to the structure, operating procedures and duties of LRECs. According to Article 26, paragraph 1, LRECs can consist of a minimum of seven and a maximum of fifteen members. The same article also defines two different LRECs: Clinical Research Review Committees (CRRCs) and Bioavailability-Bioequivalence Research Review Committees (BBRRCs); the former group of committees is authorized to review all kinds of clinical research other than bioavailability-bioequivalence studies, which are required to be reviewed by the latter group of LRECs. LRECs established in a university are to be approved by the rector of the institution, whereas LRECs in other state healthcare institutions are to be approved by the general secretary of the institution.

186. Paragraph 6 of Article 26 states that all LRECs are required to have at least three members who are not employed in the institution where the committees' secretarial office resides; by the same token, paragraphs 7 and 8 respectively state that an LREC member cannot serve in any other LRECs and that senior administrators of the institutions cannot serve in LRECs, respectively. These restrictions have probably been placed to facilitate objective decision-making for LRECs.

187. Paragraph 10 of the aforementioned article defines the minimum qualifications for CRRC members. Accordingly, a CRRC must include specialist physicians (no exact number is stated), and preferably, these physicians should have participated in research conducted in line with the requirements of GCP. In addition, CRRCs must also contain a pharmacologist (either a pharmacist with a doctoral degree in this field or a medical doctor with a specialist degree or doctoral degree in pharmacology), a member with a doctoral degree in biostatistics or a public health specialist, an expert working in the field of biomedical engineering (or, if no such person is available, a biophysicist or a physiologist), an attorney, a lay member and, if possible, a medical ethicist (defined as a specialist or a someone with a doctoral degree in the field) and a clinical pharmacist.

188. The member requirements for BBRRCs as defined in the next paragraph of Article 26 are also very similar; the only exception is the lack of a biomedical engineer/physiologist/biophysicist member for this latter group of LRECs.

D. Other Types of Ethics Committees

189. The other most common type of ethics committees in Turkey is known as Animal Research Local Ethics Committees. These have been operating since the enactment of a specific regulation on the issue in the second half of 2006, entitled 'Regulation on Operating Procedures of Animal Research Ethics Committees' (*Hay van Deneyleri Etik Kurullarının Çalışma Usul ve Esaslarina Dair Yönetmelik*). Similar to the previous RDT issued in 1993, this regulation also defines a Central Animal Research Ethics Committee that sits in Ankara and local animal research ethics committees operating under its supervision. The Regulation defines the tasks of these committees which review animal research protocols.

Part II. The Physician–Patient Relationship

Chapter 1. General Description

§1. Rights and Duties of Physicians and Patients

I. The Physician–Patient Relationship

A. Introduction

190. There is no specific legislation in Turkey regulating the physician–patient relationship. However, several different laws and regulations include provisions that may be classified under this rubric. LPOMRA *(Tababet ve Şuabatı Sanatlarının Tarz-ı İcrasına Dair Kanun,* 1928), MDR *(Tıbbi Deontoloji Tüzüğü* – 1960) Law on the Transplantation, Grafting and Storage of Organs *(Organ ve Doku Alınması Aşılanması ve Saklanması Hakkında Kanun,* 1979), RPR *(Hasta Hakları Yönetmeliği,* 1998) address important issues within the context of the patient–physician relationship. The Turkish Penal Code also includes several provisions that could be considered part of this rubric.

B. The Duty of Care for Patients

191. Turkish law defines the physician–patient relationship as a contractually based relationship, though some procedures (such as organ transplantation, abortion and in vitro fertilization) are performed according to legislation regulating these specific procedures. Certain provisions of the MDR, RPR and LPOMRA also apply.

C. Respect for the Patient's Personhood

192. MDR (1960) includes provisions that apply to the patient–physician relationship. Article 2 of this regulation states that the physicians' and dentists' principal responsibility is to respect the health, life and personhood of each individual and provide due care. Physicians are required to act according to this provision regardless of the race, gender, language, religion or political views of the patient. Article 3 of the same regulation states that unless there is a matter of force majeure, all physicians are obligated to provide first aid in emergency cases.

D. Respect for the Private Life of the Patient

193. Article 4 of the MDR states that a patient's confidential information may not be disclosed to third parties. The disclosure of a patient's identity in scientific meetings and publications is also prohibited. Article 17 states that the private and family life of the patient should not be subject to interference. These two articles aim to provide respect for the private life of the patient.

E. The Right of the Patient to Choose His/Her Physician

194. Article 5 of the MDR states that the patient may freely choose his/her physician and that the patient can exercise this right in the healthcare institutions he/she can access within legal limits.

F. Informing the Patient

195. Article 14 of the MDR emphasizes that the physician should inform the patient of the diagnosis and of the treatment that will be provided. Although the limits of disclosure and how information is to be delivered to the patient are not defined, circumstances where disclosure may not be provided have been addressed in this article. For example, information may be withheld if the patient might be harmed upon learning his/her diagnosis. The article further states that if a patient has been diagnosed with a disease associated with a bad prognosis, and if the specific person to be informed of this prognosis has not been nominated by the patient, then the information may be disclosed to the patient's family. This article allows disclosure of patient information to family members unless the patient has stated otherwise beforehand. This provision is open to criticism, since it may give rise to situations incompatible with respect for the patient's privacy.[51]

G. Refusal of the Physician to Provide Medical Care for the Patient

196. Article 18 of the MDR prohibits the refusal to provide medical care. This provision applies to all physicians (serving in either the public or private sector) in case of medical emergencies, whereas in other conditions it mainly applies to physicians serving in the public sector. Article 19 clarifies the requirements when a physician wishes to terminate the physician–patient relationship before completing the treatment process. It states that the physician must inform the patient before termination in enough time for another physician to be found who can resume the treatment process. However, if the illness endangers the life or health of the patient, then

51. G. Sert, Tıp Etiği ve Tıp Hukuku Açısından Sağlık Hizmetlerinde Mahremiyet Hakkı Kavramı (*The Right to Privacy in Health Care Services in the Perspective of Medical Ethics and Medical Law*). Doktora Tezi (*Ph.D. Thesis, soon to be published*), Marmara Üniversitesi Sağlık Bilimleri Enstitüsü, İstanbul, 2007. Danışman: (*Mentor*) Şefik Görkey, s. 87.

the physician may not withhold his/her services before another physician actually takes over the responsibility or treatment. Also, when another physician starts to provide care for the patient, the relevant documents must be provided to the new physician.

H. Consultation

197. The consultation process, where the opinion of a physician other than the primary treating physician is sought, and issues regarding this process have been addressed in the MDR. Article 24 states that when a patient demands a consultation from another physician, the primary physician should respect such a request. However, if the primary physician demands a consultation from another physician but the patient does not agree to this consultation, then the primary physician may stop providing healthcare for the particular patient.

Article 25 emphasizes that during consultation the physicians should share information with the patient and patient's relatives and information should be shared in a manner that can be understood by a layperson. Article 26 states that the results of the consultation should be noted and should be signed by the physicians participating in the consultation process. In addition, a physician's manners that can negatively affect the patient and the relatives are to be avoided during the consultation process.

If the consulting physician suggests that the treatment of the primary physician is not appropriate, then he/she is required to record this opinion in the file, but the consulting physician should not interfere with the treatment process, as stated in Article 27.

The consulting physician and primary physician administering the treatment may express different views on how to proceed, and the patient may choose to proceed with the consulting physician's recommendation. In such a case, if the primary physician insists on following his/her own judgment, then he/she may end his/her relationship with the patient, as addressed in Article 28.

Article 29 states that the consulting physician may not undertake the position of primary physician unless the patient demands this. The same article states that the consulting physician may not visit the patient without the permission of the primary physician.

Article 30 of the Regulation includes provisions for consultation fees. It states that the treating physician and the consulting physician should assess fees independently and that assessing a unified fee and then later splitting these fees between the physicians is prohibited.

I. Physician Fees and Related Issues

198. Article 28 of the TPAL lists the determination of medical fees among the duties of the Board of Chamber of Physicians. Thus, the board may determine the limits of physician service fees. Once the tariff is determined, it must then be approved by the TPA and submitted to the Ministry of Health. As stated above, the board resolves patient–member physician conflicts by way of negotiation, considering the dignity of the profession, the severity of the disease and the effort needed to provide healthcare service, or by assigning a referee to decide on the matter. If the matter cannot be resolved by these methods, the board may demand written statements regarding the conflict from the physician and then notify the HDB (*see also* paragraphs 108–119).

199. MDR includes provisions on physician fees. Article 31 states that the physician or the dentist may not provide his/her services at fees lower than those determined in the tariff, whereas Article 33 states that under certain conditions some services, though not all, may be provided for a predetermined fee. The same article addresses situations where the patient–physician relationship ends prematurely before the completion of treatment. In such cases, the physician shall receive his/her fee and expenses for his/her services until the time that the relationship ends. Accordingly, if a fee was overpaid, such as when paid in full in advance of treatment, the overpayment shall be returned to the patient. Article 35 declares that in situations of medical emergency, the physician may demand his/her fee at a later date. Article 32 suggests that it is appropriate for physicians to waive their fees when providing medical services to their colleagues and/or the spouses or other relatives of the colleagues (such as those whom the colleague is under legal obligation to look after); however, compulsory expenses may be charged.

§2. Informed Consent

I. The Legal Function of Informed Consent in Turkish Law

200. The concept of informed consent consists of disclosure and comprehension of information, and consent. An informed decision by the patient prior to medical interventions is a requirement of Turkish law. While the legislation refers to this process with the simple term 'consent', the implied nature of such consent in Turkish law is an informed one.

A. The Significance of Informed Consent for the Patient

201. Seeking the consent of the patient is required by law as a sign of respect for the personhood and freedom of the individual. The individual has the right to refuse any intervention directed towards his/her physical integrity. Medical examination and surgical intervention may also be refused on this basis. The 1982 Constitution of the Turkish Republic also forbids medical intervention without the consent of the individual, with the exception of certain situations determined in the law, as stated in the Constitution, Article 17, paragraph 2.

202. The Oviedo Convention (Convention for the Protection of Human Rights and Dignity of the Human Being with Regard to the Application of Biology and Medicine: Convention on Human Rights and Biomedicine) is binding on Turkey since it was ratified as a part of the Turkish Republic's national legislation. The Convention emphasized the significance of this consent in its Article 5.

203. In addition, the RPR states in Article 24 that medical intervention may not be performed without the consent of the patient.

II. The Criteria for Obtaining Informed Consent as Required by Turkish Law

204. In order for informed consent to be legally valid in Turkish law, it must contain three components: (1) the consenting individual must have the capacity to consent; (2) the intervention for which the consent is sought must be legal; and (3) the individual whose consent is sought must be informed.

A. Capacity to Consent

205. Turkish law requires the individual to have the capacity to consent. Such an individual must be either fully competent or have limited competency. A fully competent individual in Turkish law is an adult with discernment capacity and with no legally imposed restriction.

1. Discernment Capacity

206. According to Turkish law, lacking in discernment capacity implies irrational acts due to young age, mental disease, mental weakness, the influence of alcohol or similar reasons, as addressed in Article 13 of the Turkish Civil Code. Since discernment capacity is a relative term, the presence or lack of such capacity should be determined from actual cases.

207. Aside from young children, an individual is considered to have discernment capacity by default. This includes individuals legally restricted due to reasons other than mental disease or weakness. When individuals considered having discernment capacity claim they lack it, then the burden of proof for proving the lack of such capacity is on the claimant. Conversely, people with mental disorders and mental weaknesses are, by default, considered lacking such capacity, with the burden of proof on the party claiming to have discernment capacity.

2. Adulthood (Maturity)

208. Another requirement for the existence of legal capacity is maturity (i.e., the person should be an adult to have legal capacity). An adult is someone who has attained the age minimum accepted by the law for reaching maturity or who is considered to have attained this age due to other reasons (such as marriage). This age minimum has been set as 18 years in Turkish law. Adulthood commences after fully completing 18 years of age, and if other requirements are also fulfilled, then the individual has legal capacity, as stated in Article 11 of the Turkish Civil Code.

3. No Legally Imposed Restriction

209. Legally restricted individuals are persons whose authority to engage in a legal process has been limited due to reasons stated in the law, such as mental disease, mental weakness, alcohol abuse, thriftlessness, leading an unacceptable style of life and conviction of a criminal offence. These reasons have been defined in detail in Articles 405–408 of the Turkish Civil Code.

210. A person possessing legal capacity may freely decide on medical intervention. Individuals lacking discernment may not act on their own in legal processes and are considered totally incompetent individuals who do not have the authority to decide on medical intervention. Instead, their legal representative (custodian or legal guardian) may decide on their behalf. Such individuals may be subject to medical intervention if their legal representative consents to the procedure.

B. Lawfulness of the Medical Intervention

211. The medical intervention must be lawful before consent is sought. Consent obtained for interventions prohibited by law is not valid. The RPR also includes a clear provision on this issue in its Article 28.

C. Informing the Patient

212. Disclosure of information is another requirement for consent to be considered legally valid. Disclosure has several elements, as detailed below.

1. The Scope of the Disclosure

213. Information to be disclosed should include the diagnosis and information on suggested medical interventions or treatment methods.

a. Information on Diagnosis

214. All information pertaining to the disease (its characteristics, aetiology and effects) should be disclosed. Transmission of such knowledge obtained via physical examination is known as 'diagnosis disclosure'.[52] It is permissible, however, to withhold information about fatal diseases or diseases that cannot be cured with current medical knowledge.[53]

b. Information about the Medical Intervention

215. The physician has to inform the patient about the proposed medical intervention. The benefits, as well as the risks of the intervention and possible loss of function or disability that may occur as a result of a surgical method, should be disclosed. This process is known as 'risk disclosure'.[54,55] It should be noted that such disclosure is among the controversial topics concerning the information to be disclosed about medical intervention.

216. The Turkish High Court of Appeals has addressed the issue in one of its verdicts: 'Since medical interventions and other actions to be carried out by the physician is concerned with the health and physical integrity of the individual, the authority to decide on such interventions belongs to the patient, and not to the physician.'[56]

217. If there are alternative treatment methods available, the physician has to inform the patient about them with regard to their benefits and risks and thus give the patient the chance to make a choice. There are interventions where disclosure of risks should be more detailed; in particular, when there is no medical necessity (such as plastic surgery interventions), or where no therapeutic benefit is expected for the individual (as in the case of transplantation donors).[57] Disclosure under such circumstances should contain the remotest risks of the proposed interventions.

2. The Content of the Disclosure

218. Until the RPR was issued on 1 August 1998, there were no legislations defining the limits of disclosure for general medical practice. However, some provisions included in certain legislations addressing specific procedures (such as the LOT) had statements that could offer guidance on the issue.[58] RPR provisions on disclosure are a milestone in that aspect. Article 15 of the Regulation states that the patient should be given information about his/her medical condition, interventions planned to be performed, benefits of such interventions and their probable risks, other alternative methods of treatment and the course and prognosis of treatment.

52. Ayan, *supra* para. 45, n. 1, s. 71.
53. *Ibid.*, s. 81.
54. *Ibid.*, s. 72.
55. Hakeri, *supra* para. 96, n. 2, ss 121–122.
56. Yargıtay 4. Hukuk Dairesi (*High Court of Appeals, 4. Judicial Law Office*), verdict No. 2541, dated 7 Mar. 1977.
57. Ayan, *supra* para. 45, n. 1, s. 77.
58. G. Sert, Hasta Hakları Uluslararası Bildirgeler ve Tıp Etiği Açısından (*Patient Rights from the Perspective of International Documents and Medical Ethics*) (İstanbul, Babil Yayınları 2004), s. 227.

Revised version of Patient Rights Regulation (PRR) (2014) Article 15 is enriched/enlarged with the content of information. Due to the revision, information given to patients should include aetiology and prognosis of the disease, by whom, where and how the medical intervention will be performed and possible duration, other diagnosis and treatment options, risks and benefits and possible results to patients' health, possible complications, risks and benefits in case of treatment refusal, specialities of drugs/medicaments, risky lifestyle for his/her health and to reach medical support. In addition, Article 18 states that information should be given in a manner in which the patient can understand, without leaving any doubt and in accordance with the psychological condition of the patient. Furthermore, information should be free of medical terms as much as possible.

219. Professional Code of Ethics of TPA also addresses the content of disclosure in its provisions. The content and the standards of disclosure, although not definite, have been determined in Article 26 of the Codes.

a. Extending the Scope of Disclosure

220. Some authors defend that the characteristics of the intervention to be performed should be the basis for determining the scope of disclosure.[59] One of these characteristics is the urgency of the intervention.[60] Accordingly, the scope of disclosure increases as the urgency of the intervention decreases, or vice versa.[61]

221. Another factor influencing the scope of disclosure is the magnitude of risk. As the amount of risk taken with the intervention increases, the scope of disclosure should also be extended accordingly.[62] In this context, whether the probable harm that may occur will be temporary is the most important factor for determining the scope of disclosure.

222. Whether the intervention serves a therapeutic purpose is also of significance. If the intervention does not serve the purpose of direct therapeutic benefit, the scope of disclosure should be extended. Examples of such interventions include plastic surgery and sterilization procedures.[63]

223. The same principle applies to newly developed methods of treatment that have not been widely accepted. If such a treatment method is to be performed, the patient should be offered a detailed disclosure.[64]

---

59. Ayan, *supra* para. 45, n. 1, ss 75–76.
60. B. Erman, Tıbbi Müdahalenin Hukuka Uygunluğu (*Lawfulness of the Medical Intervention*), Seçkin Yayınları, Ankara, 2003, s. 111.
61. Hakeri, *supra* para. 96, n. 2, ss 124–125.
62. Erman, *supra* para. 177, n. 2, s. 111.
63. *Ibid.*, s. 111.
64. G. Sert, Hasta Hakları Uluslararası Bildirgeler ve Tıp Etiği Açısından (*Patient Rights from the Perspective of International Documents and Medical Ethics*) (Babil Yayınları İstanbul, 2004), s. 229.

224. Another situation requiring extended disclosure is the clear demand of the patient for information. However, it should be noted that the patient does not have to ask for disclosure; disclosure should be performed even when no clear demand has been made.

225. Under circumstances where the patient may have the option to choose a method of treatment from multiple options, the scope of disclosure needs to be extended. Similarly, when there is one single method of treatment available, the scope of disclosure may be narrowed.

b. Narrowing the Scope of Disclosure

226. The scope of the duty to disclose may also be narrowed in accordance with the nature of the medical intervention and according to the specific characteristics of the concrete case. In a sense, situations where the scope of disclosure may be narrowed are the opposite of cases where extended disclosure is required. For instance, when the urgency of intervention increases, the scope of disclosure may be narrowed.

227. Another example where the scope of disclosure may be narrowed in accordance with the characteristics of the concrete case is the probability of psychologically harming a patient due to a comprehensive disclosure. Such cases involve a conflict between the patient's right to self-determination and the physician's duty to protect the patient from harm or to 'do no harm'. When the harm that may come to the patient outweighs the patient's right to self-determination, the scope of disclosure may be limited for the good of the patient. This approach is known as 'therapeutic privilege' and a provision compatible with this approach is also included in MDR's Article 14, which states that the physician is not under an obligation to offer a detailed disclosure under the conditions described above. A similar provision has also been included in RPR in Article 19, which affirms that the physician may not inform the patient when the disclosure of diagnosis may affect the course of the disease in a negative way.[65] However, if the patient openly demands information, the physician should then disclose the facts that may have a negative effect.[66]

c. Conditions Where the Duty to Disclose May Be Entirely Abolished

228. It is claimed that under certain conditions, the duty to disclose is abolished.[67,68] Some of these conditions are entirely related to the subjective characteristics or attitudes of the patient.

---

65. Hakeri, *supra* para. 96, n. 2, ss 141–142.
66. G. Sert, Hasta Hakları Uluslararası Bildirgeler ve Tıp Etiği Açısından (*Patient Rights from the Perspective of International Documents and Medical Ethics*) (Babil Yayınları İstanbul, 2004), s. 230; Ayan, *supra* para. 45, n. 1, s. 78.
67. Ayan, *supra* para. 45, n. 1, ss 78–79.
68. Hakeri, *supra* para. 96, n. 2, ss 137–139.

229. The patient, based on his/her free will, may waive his/her right to be informed.[69] However, when such waiver is not based on the free will of the patient and there is coercion or deception involved, the consent is not legally valid. The patient waiving the right to be informed should clearly declare this; however, an implied (not openly stated) declaration may also be sufficient. RPR also includes a provision which recognizes this right that is commonly referred to as the 'right not to know'.

It is defended that under certain conditions (as in newly developed treatment methods that have not been widely accepted), it should not be possible to waive the right to be informed. Similarly, it is also asserted that the legal representative of the patient with no discernment capacity should not be allowed to waive such right.[70]

230. The immediate necessity of intervention is also one of the conditions that entirely abolishes the duty to disclose. When the intervention must be performed immediately in order to prevent harm or to save the life of the patient, the disclosure may not be performed.[71] The classic example of such cases is the situation of individuals losing consciousness following a traffic accident.

231. One of the controversial situations about the duty to disclose in case of an unconscious patient involves medical conditions where the scope of the surgical intervention has to be extended. Under some exceptional situations, a need may arise to extend the scope of surgery or the type of surgery after the intervention has been initiated under general anaesthesia. As a rule, such process of extending or changing the type of surgery requires the consent of the individual. However, seeking consent may not be compulsory in conditions where it is impossible to inform the patient of the situation. The key issue here would be to determine whether such a change could be foreseen beforehand; if it can be foreseen that extending the scope of surgery will be required, then the physician should seek the consent of the patient accordingly.[72] Due to the regulation of PRR 2014, Article 31, the necessity to inform the patient in advance of medical intervention is re-emphasized. Medical intervention cannot surpass the limits of patient consent. Medical intervention should be within the limits of patients' consent unless there is a risk of organ loss. In such a situation, medical intervention can be extended/enlarged without patients' consent.

3. Executing the Duty to Disclose

232. As a rule, the duty to disclose primarily belongs to the physician. Such duty arises both from the Constitutional provisions and from the treatment contract

69. Erman, *supra* para. 177, n. 2, s. 116.
70. G. Sert, Hasta Hakları Uluslararası Bildirgeler ve Tıp Etiği Açısından (*Patient Rights from the Perspective of International Documents and Medical Ethics*) (Babil Yayınları İstanbul, 2004), s. 231; Ayan, *supra* para. 45, n. 1, s. 79.
71. Erman, *supra* para. 177, n. 2, s. 111.
72. Ayan, *supra* para. 45, n. 1, s. 80.

imposed by the Obligations Law. The physician owes no such duty under conditions where the duty to disclose is abolished; however, determining these conditions is the physician's responsibility.[73] If the intervention is to be performed by a team, then it could be argued that all the physicians in the team should disclose information relevant to their field of speciality, but it could also be possible for the leader of such a team to perform disclosure alone.[74]

233. As a rule, the patient himself/herself should be informed. When the patient lacks discernment capacity, determining whether such lack of capacity is permanent gains significance. If the capacity has been lost for a temporary reason, such as a traffic accident or substance overdose, interventions medically required to protect the health and life of the individual may be carried out without disclosure and consent. The immediate necessity of the situations would justify such an act. However, when the individual permanently lacks discernment capacity, then information has to be disclosed to the legal representative of the person. If the legal representative is unavailable or seeking his consent is not possible, the physician may intervene on the basis of immediate necessity.

a. The Timing of Disclosure

234. The purpose and content of disclosure require this duty to be performed prior to consent. The patient should be given the time to evaluate the information that has been transferred. He/she may also need time to consult relatives or other close acquaintances.[75,76]

b. The Manner in Which Disclosure Is Made

235. The style and the manner in which information is delivered are important. The physician should inform his/her patient in accordance with the individual's education level. Subjective conditions such as the age and health status of the patient should be considered. The medical knowledge should be delivered in words the patient can understand. Article 18 of RPR also contains a provision compatible with this approach.

4. The Type of Disclosure

236. There is no general rule for the type of informed consent in Turkish law; it may be obtained in written or oral form in general.[77] However, RPR's Article 28 emphasizes that the type of consent may be significant under certain circumstances

73. *Ibid.*, s. 82.
74. *Ibid.*, s. 82.
75. *Ibid.*, s. 83.
76. Hakeri, *supra* para. 96, n. 2, s. 130.
77. Erman, *supra* para. 177, n. 2, s. 124.

defined by law. For instance, the LPOMRA necessitates written consent for all surgical procedures. The LOT (*Organ ve Doku Alınması, Saklanması, Aşılanması ve Nakli Hakkında Kanun*) and the Regulation on the Practice and Control of Therapeutic Abortion and Sterilization Services (*Rahim Tahliyesi ve Sterilizasyon Hizmetlerinin Yürütülmesi ve Denetlenmesine İlişkin Tüzük)* also state that these procedures require written consent. It is defended in Turkish legal doctrine that oral disclosure is more appropriate for the purpose served by disclosure.[78] It is also argued that following oral disclosure, it will be useful to document this in written form, for the purpose of establishing the evidence of disclosure.[79,80] Due to the amendment on 8 May 2014 of PRR Article 26, written consent of the patient should be required in foreseen incompatibility.

5. Proving Disclosure

237. There is no clear provision on proving disclosure in Turkish law. The duty to disclose has two main legal grounds: The first one is the essential status of disclosure to ensure a valid consent; the other one is the treatment contract.[81] The right to self-determination of the individual, which is under legal protection in the Constitution, necessitates the existence of consent of the individual if the medical intervention is to be considered lawful. When the duty to disclose has not been carried out, the consent is not valid, which in turn implies that the physician's intervention has not been carried out on lawful grounds. The act becomes unlawful. The burden of proof for showing the lawfulness of such act belongs to the physician claiming lawfulness, which means that he/she should be able to demonstrate that disclosure has taken place.

238. The second legal basis justifying the duty to disclose is the treatment contract. On this basis, the duty is an obligation arising from the contract between the patient and the physician. The party which claims that such an obligation has not been carried out by the other party has the burden of proof and has to demonstrate that the other party did not act as required by the contract.

Both of these legal grounds can be defended in Turkish law. The first solution defends the interest of the patient, whereas the second does so for the physician. If the obligation to disclose information is only evaluated on the basis of the contract, then it will be appropriate to leave the burden of proof to the party making a claim.

---

78. Oral disclosure is usually the preferred method of disclosure in Turkey; however, efforts for additional written disclosure for supporting oral information are also becoming popular. *See* T. Güven. *Hastaların Aydınlatılmasında Yazılı Bilgilendirme Yönteminin Kullanılması: Benin Prostat Hiperplazisi ve Prostat Kanseri Hastaları ile bir Çalışma (The Use of Written Disclosure in Informed Consent: A Study with Benign Prostate Hyperplasia and Prostate Cancer Patients).* Basılmamiş Tıpta Uzmanlık Tezi *(Unpublished Specialty Thesis in Medicine).* Kocaeli Üniversitesi Tıp Fakültesi Tıp Tarihi ve Deontoloji Anabilim Dalı. Kocaeli 2002. Danışman *(Mentor)* Nermin Ersoy, s. 33.
79. Ayan, *supra* para. 45, n. 1, ss 84–85.
80. Hakeri, *supra* para. 96, n. 2, ss 133–134.
81. Ayan, *supra* para. 45, n. 1, s. 86.

However, in order to protect the patient, who is by default in a weaker status than the physician is, the correct solution will be to leave the burden of proof to the physician.[82]

III. Medical Interventions That May Be Carried Out Without Consent

239. Article 17 of the Constitution implies that certain medical interventions may be carried out without the consent of the individual. Laws allow such procedures on the basis of protecting public benefit and health and ensuring justice. Articles 67, 72–75, 88, 90, 101, 103, 107, 112, 119, 284, 287, 288 and 291 of the Common Health Law *(Umumi Hıfzıssıhha Kanunu)* and Articles 7 and 16 of The Law on the Eradication of Malaria *(Sıtmanın İmhası Hakkında Kanun)* include examples of such exceptional situations.[83]

240. The Turkish Penal Code also includes provisions on compulsory treatment.[84] Article 188 states that individuals engaging in substance abuse must be treated. Accordingly, such persons have to act in accordance with the requirements of treatment and controlled freedom provided in the appropriate institution. During this period, a social service worker will be assigned to guide the person and offer counselling on how to cease substance abuse. If the person fails to act in accordance with these requirements, he/she will be convicted and the sanction imposed by the Code will be applied.

241. Article 109 of Law No. 5271 on Penal Trials (*Ceza Muhakemeleri Kanunu*), which replaced the former Law No. 1412 on Penal Trial Procedures (Ceza Muhakemeleri Usulü Kanunu) following its publication on 17 December 2004 in the Official Journal, states that when one of the reasons for arrest is present, the individuals may be placed under judiciary control instead of being placed under arrest. It is stated that particularly for individuals engaging in substance and alcohol abuse, several precautions may be taken, including diagnostic and treatment procedures and admission to a hospital for stay. In addition, Article 227, paragraph 8 of the Turkish Penal Code, states that victims of prostitution will be subjected to treatment.[85]

242. Physical examination: Through physical examinations carried out on the suspect or accused, the Law on Penal Trials *(Ceza Muhakemeleri Kanunu)* aims to provide evidence of a crime, and to take blood or similar biological samples from the body, such as hair, saliva and nails (Articles 75–81). In order to clarify the practices related to physical examination, the 'Regulation on Physical Examination,

82. *Ibid.*
83. Hakeri, *supra* para. 96, n. 2, ss 221–223.
84. Erman, *supra* para. 177, n. 2, s. 175.
85. Y. Ünver, *Avrupa, Biyo-Hukuk Sözleşmesinin Türk Hukukuna Etkileri (The Effects of European Bioethics Convention on Turkish Law).* Kamu Hukuku Arşivi, Akademik Araştırma ve Dayanışma Derneği Yayını Ed. M. Avcı, 8: 2. Kasım 2005, ss 182–198.

Genetic Investigations and Determination of Physical Identity in Criminal Procedure' was enacted.[86] In this Regulation, physical examination is defined as 'medical examination of the body'. The Regulation defines internal body examination as the examination of the head, chest and abdominal cavities and subcutaneous tissues. The Regulation defines external body examination as superficial medical examination of the outer surface of the body and the ear, nose and mouth. In the Regulation, imaging examinations are accepted as external body examinations. It should be noted that the external body examination in Law on Penal Trials is not included in the law. Law on Penal Trials arranged the physical examination of the accused and suspects and the victim in separate articles. In both cases, there are some differences, although similar conditions for examination are sought.

243. *Decision-making authority medical examination:* In order to obtain evidence, a physical examination may be requested at the request of the Prosecutor or the victim, either by a judge or court decision or by a court or judge's ex officio decision. According to the same article, a physical examination may be requested by a prosecutor's decision (Law on Penal Trials Article 75). The same conditions were foreseen for the examination of the victim. However, if the victim gives consent, the decision of the judge or prosecutor is not required. The Regulation stipulates that both the suspect and the accused's request for external physical examination may be requested by the public prosecutor or the judicial police (Article 5).

244. *Give no harm to the health of suspected, accused or other persons:* The internal examination of the accused or suspect should not be a danger to the person's health (Law on Penal Trials Article 75). Internal body examination of the victim, accused or suspect should not be a danger to the person's health (Law on Penal Trials Article 75). Surgical intervention cannot be performed during the examinations to be made to the victim (Law on Penal Trials Article 76). There is no explanation in the Law on Penal Trials on what to understand from the danger of harm to health. The Regulation used a clearly predictable loss statement. The doctrine of Turkish law does not limit the scope of giving harm to health, to cause pathological conditions. Although it does not require treatment, movements that cause abrasion, swelling and bruises, or disrupt the nervous system, damaging mental health are also considered as giving harm to the health.

245. *Physical examination can only be performed by the physician*: According to the law, internal physical examination can be performed by physicians and healthcare professionals. The Regulation states that both internal and external physical examinations can be performed only by the physician. According to the Regulation, the physical examination is a medical examination and the examination should be carried out in accordance with the medical rules. It should be acknowledged that performing medical examinations by a medical professional is necessary to respect the integrity of the person. The physicians performing the examination are obliged to act in accordance with the principles of professional ethics and medical deontology.

86. RG: 1.6.2005, RG No. 25832.

246. Suspicious, accused or other persons who do not give consent: The Code of Criminal Procedure did not regulate the procedure to be followed if the suspect or the accused refused physical examination. It is argued that this law does not allow forcible examination in these cases. The Regulation foresees that although there are other conditions related to physical examination, the accused or suspect may be forced if he does not give consent to the examination (Article 18).

According to the Regulation, both the accused and the suspects and other persons can be examined by non-invasive imaging methods by healthcare professionals. Performing an internal body examination to obtain evidence, even for the purpose of providing justice or social order, may cause problems in terms of compliance with *giving no harm* principle.

247. Article 26 of RPR necessitates consulting minors or legally restricted individuals about their opinions on the medical interventions to be performed on them. However, this provision is still not exactly in accordance with the Turkish Civil Code, which states that minors having discernment capacity (limited competence) can exercise their rights strictly related to their personal being without permission (*see also* paragraphs 208 et seq.).

248. Another noteworthy (albeit indirectly related to the topic) provision has been included in RPR's Article 25, which limits the right to refuse treatment in situations where a vital organ is in danger or when a life-threatening medical situation is present.

249. Forced retaining of substance addicts and mental patients in health institutions: The law stipulates that in some cases people may be forced to undergo treatment. These exceptions include the forced admission or treatment of some mentally ill or substance addicts. The Constitutional Law and the European Convention on Human Rights contain framework provisions on the forced retaining of drug addicts and mentally ill patients to institutions. Article 432 of the Turkish Civil Law includes provisions on implementation. According to Article 432 of the Turkish Civil Law, it is stated that a restriction of freedom for protection decision can be taken in cases of mental illness, mental weakness, alcohol or drug addiction, severe infectious disease or vagrants which constitutes a danger to the society. The aim is to prevent the persons in this situation from harming themselves or others by placing them in a health institution which is suitable for their education and rehabilitation where they cannot be otherwise protected.

250. In order to prevent violations of rights in this regard, the relevant conditions are stated in the TMK. In the absence of one of these conditions, the decision to restrict the freedom of the person for protection purposes will not be taken. Public officials who encounter the aforementioned situations in the performance of their duties may request to limit the person's freedom for protection. In addition, the legal representative or relatives of the person may make such a request. These requests can be made before or after the person is placed in the institution. Decisions of referral to the health institution, placement in the institution, detention and removal from the institution are made by the court.

251. In order for such a decision to be made, the person should be an adult. It should be determined by the board report that the person to whom the protection decision is made for protection purposes has mental illness and that it presents a danger of self-harm or harm to others. In order to take a decision on the limitation of freedom for protection purposes, the person must not be protected by any other method or measure.

252. Mandatory vaccination in children: In Turkey, according to the Expanded Immunization Program, some vaccines (polio, rubella, mumps, diphtheria, Haemophilus, chickenpox, hepatitis A and hepatitis B, tuberculosis, pneumococcal, influenza, measles, whooping cough) are required. Since some parents did not want the prescribed vaccinations, legal debates have started as to whether childhood vaccinations are compulsory or not. Information on vaccination rejections has been on the national agenda since 2010.[87] Judicial decisions have been effective in determining the legal situation regarding compulsory vaccination of children in our country.

253. Until 2015, if the parent refused to vaccinate their children, the Ministry of Health reported the situation to the Provincial Directorate of Family and Social Policies. Thereupon Provincial Directorate of Family and Social Policies requested protection measures under the Child Protection Law to ensure that the child is vaccinated. In these cases, the Provincial Directorate of Family and Social Policies argued that the parent's rejection of the vaccine was contrary to the child's best interests. Although the risks of non-vaccination of children in terms of public health are mentioned in the cases, they are not subject to decisions.

254. In these decisions, the High Court of Appeals emphasized that it was essential to obtain consent after the individual was informed that the vaccine was a medical intervention and pointed out that the decision-making authority on behalf of the child lies with the parents. The Supreme Court did not find it appropriate for the child's best interests to refuse the vaccination without giving a reason despite the fact that the parents were informed of a decision. The High Court of Appeals ruled that the child could be vaccinated despite the family's refusal. The Constitutional Court noted that in cases of emergency, the Constitution allows only by legislations or where the life of the individual is in danger, interference can be made without the consent of the individual. In this context, it has been decided that the child cannot be vaccinated because there is no law that allows the vaccination to be administered without the consent of the individual and the vaccine does not contain an emergency. In the following years, the Constitutional Court made similar decisions on vaccination. In fact, the Constitutional Court has pointed out the necessity of a regulation on this issue.[88] Following this decision of the Constitutional Court, the

87. G. Sert et al. Türkiye'de Çocuklar için Zorunlu Aşılama Uygulamaları ile İlgili Yargı Kararlarının Tıp Etiği ve Hukuku Açısından İncelenmesi (*Court Decisions of Compulsory Vaccination of Children in Turkey. An Ethical Legal Evaluation*). V. National Veterinary History and Professional Symposium 25–27 May. 2016 Bursa., Abstract Book, p. 52.
88. Constitutional Court's Decision RG: 24 Dec. 2015.

High Court of Appeals rejected such requests based on the Constitutional Court's decision. After the Constitutional Court's decision, TPA proposed to amend the law. The proposal prepared within this scope is recommended to be amended by the Turkish Penal Code and the General Health Law. This issue is still on the country's agenda.

IV. Informed Consent in Research

255. *See* paragraphs 375–376.

§3. Duty of Medical Secrecy and Privacy

256. Article 134 of the Turkish Penal Code does not specifically address exceptions with regard to the violation of the confidentiality of private life. However, the Code defines situations where penal sanction will not be applicable. Commission of an act that can violate the confidentiality of private life will not constitute an offence if that act has been defined in a law article. For example, General Health Law *(Umumi Hıfzıssıhha Kanunu)* requires compulsory notification of certain communicable diseases. Notification of the relevant authorities on the grounds of this law does not constitute an offence with regard to professional secrecy. Article 280 of the Turkish Penal Code requires healthcare professionals to notify of any criminal offence without exception. Accordingly, healthcare professionals are obligated to report a crime during the course of their duty, and they cannot be held responsible for violating it under such circumstances.[89]

257. Patient information can be disclosed upon the request of a competent authority. In cases that are being examined by a court, patient information can be provided to the court upon request. However, if a healthcare professional is requested to testify in court, he or she may refuse to testify. This testimonial privilege is justified on the grounds described by the Law on Civil Trials *(Hukuk Muhakemeleri Kanunu)* and the Law on Penal Trials *(Ceza Muhakemeleri Kanunu).* Some authors suggest that this should be interpreted in the narrow sense, claiming that the healthcare professional has to refuse to testify and not refusing to testify would constitute an offence.[90] However, if the patient requests the healthcare professional's testimony, then the professional has to testify in court.

258. If withholding confidential patient information will violate the healthcare professional's or a third party's rights, then information may be disclosed. For example, if the healthcare professional will be subject to criminal prosecution in the case of not disclosing patient information, then the professional may disclose this

---

89. S. Karasu, *Hekimin Sır Saklama Yükümlülüğü (Physician's Duty to Maintain Confidentiality).* M.Ü. Sosyal, *Bilimler Enstitüsü Hukuk Anabilim Dalı Özel Hukuk Bilim Dalı Yüksek Lisans Tezi (Unpublished M. Sc. Thesis)* İstanbul, 2005. Danışman: *(Mentor)* Doç. Dr Serap Helvacı, ss 65–66.
90. Donay, *supra* para. 73, n. 1, s. 161.

information. Patient information that poses a risk to another person's life or that endangers the community's health can be disclosed to relevant parties. The Professional Code of Ethics of TPA also allows disclosure of patient information under similar conditions.

§4. Complaints

259. The patient's right to complain has been recognized in the Regulation on Patients' Rights. The Ministry of Health also issued a Directive on 15 October 2003 entitled 'Directive on Implementation of Patient Rights' *(Hasta Hakları Uygulama Yönergesi)*. Another set of directives serving the same purpose was issued on 26 July 2005. These directives serve as the basis for patient rights units established in public sector hospitals. The directives state that patient complaints are to be submitted to these units. These complaints are evaluated within the framework defined by the directives, and the patients are informed with regard to the result of the evaluation process.

§5. Access to Medical Records

I. The Obligation to Keep Medical Records

260. Several Turkish laws include provisions on the obligation to record patient information. The requirement for keeping medical records is stated in Article 72 of the LPOMRA *(Tababet ve Şuabatı Sanatlarının Tarz-ı İcrasına Dair Kanun)* issued on 14 April 1928. According to this article, recording the patient's name and identity is compulsory.

261. The Secondary Regulation on Private Hospitals *(Özel Hastaneler Yönetmeliği)* (RPH), issued on 27 March 2002, imposes obligations for maintaining patient protocol records, opening a new file for each patient, recording information about patient's health status (diagnosis, treatment, tests, etc.), as stated in Article 48. In addition, Article 34 of RPH states that photographs taken for the purpose of scientific research for the preparation of instructional material or for diagnostic purposes can also be maintained in the archives. Article 50 is entitled 'Maintaining Records on Computers' and allows all kinds of recording and related processes to be carried out on computers.

262. The Regulation on the Administration of Inpatient Health Care Institutions (RAIHI) *(Yataklı Tedavi Kurumları İşletme Yönetmeliği)* has been amended twice, in 1983 and in 2005. This regulation also includes provisions about patient records and the archiving process, detailed in Articles 66–70. In the same regulation, maintaining records containing patient data (such as clinical, physical and laboratory findings and the documents in which they should be recorded) are addressed in Articles 71–76, whereas Articles 81–87 describe the data recording and other related processes for discharging patients and procedures to be followed when a patient dies in an inpatient health institution. Article 49 states that it is compulsory for hospitals to establish an archive for maintaining the medical records of patients. Accordingly, such archives are to be utilized to provide the necessary documents that can be requested by the patients. Recording and archiving patient data and ensuring the confidentiality of such data have also been defined as a legal liability for the individual or the institution carrying out the medical interventions.

II. Confidentiality of Medical Records

263. Turkish Obligations Law (*Borçlar Kanunu*) imposes responsibilities to the institution or individual providing healthcare for ensuring the confidentiality of medical data. Accordingly, the treatment contract, when evaluated within the context of a contract of mandate, imposes obligations on the institution or the individual providing healthcare to take the necessary precautions.

III. Ownership of Medical Records

264. While the problem about the ownership of medical data has not been precisely answered in Turkish law, there are more clear provisions about access to medical records.[91] One of the important issues on this topic involves handling the records and documents recorded by the physician or provided by the patient during the treatment process. What is to be done for such material after the contractual relationship between the physician and the patient ends is controversial. Such material can be evaluated in two different groups. Documents handed to the physician by the patient remain under the ownership of the patient. The physician is obligated to maintain such data and to return them when demanded by the patient. This obligation can be evaluated within the context of 'the duty of the proxy to return what has been taken', as stated in the Obligations Law (*Borçlar Kanunu*), Article 508. In contrast, ownership of the documents personally prepared by the physician during treatment belongs to the physician. The patient has no ownership over such documents. However, whether the patient has the right to see and demand the transfer of ownership is open to debate. Three different opinions are offered on the issue.[92] The first view claims that since the documents prepared by the physician contain information based on the personal opinions of the physician, the physician may not allow the patient to see them. The second view holds that all documents related to the patient should be given to the patient. According to this view, 'the duty to return' mentioned above is also connected with the duty to maintain confidentiality and returning such documents will serve to keep the confidentiality of patient information in the best way. The third view holds that the decision should be made according to the balance between the interest of the patient and interest of the physician. Therefore, documents in which the interest of the patient outweighs other concerns

---

91. G. Sert, Hasta Hakları Uluslararası Bildirgeler ve Tıp Etiği Açısından (*Patient Rights from the Perspective of International Documents and Medical Ethics*) (Babil Yayınları İstanbul, 2004), s. 135.
92. Ayan, *supra* para. 45, n. 1, ss 96–97.

(such as documents that will be helpful for the future healthcare of the patient) should be given to the patient on demand. This view holds that in the case where the interest of the physician and of the patient is of equal weight, the patient should only have the right to see the documents, such as the surgery protocol and disease history, but should not be allowed to demand the transfer of their ownership. Finally, for documents which can only be of benefit to the physician, it is suggested that the patient should not be allowed to see them.

265. The third view summarized above is recently emphasized in Turkish legal doctrine.[93] However, it should also be noted that Article 52 of RPH lists the documents that should be provided to patients free of charge. The documents listed include the list of drugs and other related materials charged to the patient, laboratory results and X-rays (on condition that the master copies of the documents are maintained for cases undergoing forensic investigation), prescriptions of the drugs purchased from pharmacies outside the hospital, documents and laboratory findings stating the patient's health status, the diagnosis and the course of the disease, diagnostic tests and treatment procedures and the hospital discharge note prepared by the physician. The requirement for the compulsory provision of such documents shows that the property of these documents belongs to the patient. The ownership of such records in public hospitals is not clear. However, any patient utilizing social security services should be able to receive such documents as well. The master copies of some documents may be withheld for the protection of public benefit.

IV. Accessing Medical Records

266. The RPR, in line with the fundamental patient rights defined in the Europe Declaration on Promotion of Patient Rights (Amsterdam, 1994), includes precise provisions in Article 16, under the heading of 'Examining medical records'. The right to demand correction in these records has also been recognized for patients. The Draft Law on the Protection of Personal Data also recognizes the right to demand correction and to block the access of others to such information. This Draft Law has been prepared in accordance with the European Council Convention No. 108 for the Protection of Individuals with Regard to Automatic Processing of Personal Data, which has been signed but not yet ratified by Turkey.[94]

§6. Patient Rights in Turkish Law

I. Introduction

267. Patient rights began to be debated in Turkey at the end of the 1980s. However, starting from the first years of the Turkish Republic, certain patient rights,

93. *Ibid.*, ss 96–97.
94. G. Uygur & T.Y. Sancar, *National Regulations on Ethics and Research in Turkey* 14 (European Commission Science and Society Brussels 2005).

within the context of fundamental human rights, had already been defined in the healthcare service regulations that were in force. Although certain statements found in the relevant regulations were not directly defined as 'patient rights', several patient rights (such as the right to refuse or accept medical treatment, the right to privacy, the right to equal access to healthcare, the right to choose and change the medical institution providing healthcare) were actually defined within the scope of LPOMRA (*Tababet ve Şuabatı Sanatlarının Tarz-ı İcrasına Dair Kanun*), issued in 1928, and MDR, issued in 1960.

II. Patient Rights in Turkey until the Regulation of Patient Rights in 1998

268. Shortly after the foundation of the Parliament of the Turkish Republic on 23 April 1920, the Ministry of Health and Social Welfare was founded in May 1920. With the foundation of this particular ministry, healthcare services were now considered as a duty of the state with a modern approach. This new approach intensified the efforts to overcome healthcare problems which had reached a critical level as a result of the long-lasting war. After the foundation of the Turkish Republic, the Ministry of Health and Social Welfare, responsible for all health and social services in the country, tried to take the necessary precautions along with new regulations in the field of healthcare.

269. In LPOMRA, dating from 1928, it is clearly stated that every physician and dentist should obtain the consent of the patient. General Health Law (*Umumi Hıfzıssıhha Kanunu*) dating from 1930 also addresses the rights to health and to healthcare services for every citizen of the state. The Law on the Socialization of Health Care Services, issued in 1961 (*Sağlık Hizmetlerinin Sosyalleştirilmesi Hakkında Kanun*), also defines the right to free and equal access to primary healthcare services.

270. The 1961 Turkish Constitution (the second Constitution of the Turkish Republic) was enacted shortly after and the right to health was at this time defined as a constitutional right for every Turkish citizen. The third and the final Constitution of the Turkish Republic, enacted in 1982, also recognizes the right to health, as stated in its Article 56. The same Constitution also addresses human experimentation and prohibits experimentation on human beings without the consent of the individual, as stated in Article 17. It is seen that the laws enacted after the 1982 Constitution emphasize the concepts of equality and justice in healthcare services.

271. MDR, issued in 1960, is the first text specifically addressing issues of medical deontology and ethics in Turkish legislations, and it introduces the core concepts of patient rights. However, the RPR *(Hasta Hakları Yönetmeliği)* is the most specific and current text on patient rights in Turkish law. This regulation was enacted in 1998, and the concepts and principles introduced in the text are in line with the recent international declarations on patient rights, including the Declaration of Amsterdam on Promotion of Patient Rights in Europe in 1994 and the revised Declaration of Lisbon dating from 1995. The RPR can be considered as a turning point and addresses several fundamental patient rights, such as the right of the individual to choose his/her healthcare provider, the right to be informed, the right to privacy, the right to refuse treatment. This last regulation also serves as a unifying text that combines the previous provisions on patient rights which were included in different legislations.[95,96]

III. Patient Rights as Defined in the RPR

A. *Definitions*

272. The RPR, in force since 1998, defines patient rights as the reflection of human rights in the field of healthcare and states that the purpose of the Regulation is to provide those rights in the legal framework. The term 'patient' is defined as anyone needing to utilize healthcare, as stated in Article 4 of PRR revised in 2014. Major revisions are on five subtitles: definitions, information to patients, informed consent process, responsibility of the patients and patients' rights committees.

B. *Fundamental Principles*

273. Article 5 of RPR defines the fundamental principles for the utilization of healthcare services, in line with international declarations on patient rights. Furthermore, the 1982 Constitution of the Turkish Republic emphasizes the respect for the right of the individual to live in a state of physical, psychological and social well-being and states that all individuals possess equal rights regardless of their race, language, religion, gender, political views, philosophical beliefs, economic or social status or other differences, stressing the confidentiality of the private and family life of the individual. The approach in these provisions of the Constitution is echoed in the principles outlined in RPR, and these principles can be considered to represent the adapted versions of the fundamental rights defined in the Constitution to healthcare service. In addition, Article 6 of RPR defines the right to equal and just access to healthcare.

C. *The Right to Demand Information on Healthcare Services*

274. The right to request information, as stated in Article 7 of RPR, requires the necessary precautions to be taken so that the individuals can be adequately informed

95. G. Sert, Hasta Hakları Uluslararası Bildirgeler ve Tıp Etiği Açısından *(Patient Rights from the Perspective of International Documents and Medical Ethics)* (Babil Yayınları İstanbul, 2004), s. 106.
96. A. Atac, T. Güven & C. Kilic, Patient Rights and the Current Legal Status in Turkey. 8th Congress of Balkan Military Medical Committee. 21–24 Sep. 2003, Cluj Napoca, Romania, Abstract Book, 469.

of the utilization of healthcare services. RPR also includes examples of these precautions (such as employing qualified personnel who can adequately and precisely inform patients at all times, using signposts, brochures to help patients access the proper healthcare service units easily).

D. The Right to Choose a Healthcare Institution and Healthcare Providing Personnel

275. Article 8 of RPR provides the right to choose the healthcare institution and the healthcare provider by the individuals utilizing healthcare services. The Regulation addresses issues such as changing the healthcare institution, as stated in the second paragraph of Article 8, while the right of the patients to know and choose their healthcare providers is defined in Article 9.

E. The Right to Demand the Order of Priority to Access Healthcare

276. Article 10 states that under conditions where healthcare service cannot be provided on time due to inadequate or limited sources, the patient has the right to demand the order of priority to be determined objectively, based on medical criteria.

In addition, Article 11 states that the patient has the right to demand diagnostic, therapeutic and medical care procedures in line with the state-of-the-art medical knowledge and technology.

F. The Right to Prevent Interventions Against the Individual's Life and Personhood

277. Article 12 of the Regulation aims to prevent interventions against the physical integrity of the individual. Certain interventions interfering with physical integrity are lawful even when they do not always aim to treat or protect the individual, as in the case of organ donors. Procedures for termination of pregnancy where there is no medical necessity can also be evaluated within this context. However, the law permits these procedures. Such exceptional acts which are considered lawful due to the purpose they serve, should be regulated with specific legislations, and persons involved in such interventions should be able to utilize all the rights recognized for a patient.

278. Article 13 contains provisions stating that an individual cannot waive the right to life due to medical reasons and thus the life of a patient cannot be terminated by the patient's or a third party's demand.

G. The Right to Due Care

279. The right to due care is clearly defined in Article 14 of RPR. The obligation to reduce or ameliorate the patient's pain where it is not possible to protect his/her health or save his/her life is also addressed within the context of this right.

H. The Right to Be Informed

280. The individual's right to be informed about health status and the diagnostic or therapeutic interventions to be performed in healthcare service has been defined in Article 15 of RPR. This article can be considered to clarify the debate on the scope of disclosure in Turkish law. Previously, determining the scope of disclosure was left to the legal doctrine and practice, and there were no specific regulations determining the scope of the information to be disclosed, although certain provisions of specific legislations such as the LOT (*Organ ve Doku Alınması, Saklanması, Aşılanması ve Nakli Hakkında Kanun*) and the Regulation on the Conducting and Inspection of Abortion and Sterilization Services (*Rahim Tahliyesi ve Sterilizasyon Hizmetlerinin Yürütülmesi ve Denetlenmesine İlişkin Tüzük*) included statements that could act as guidelines to healthcare professionals. Article 14 of MDR also included provisions on disclosure, and this was the only article on disclosure that could apply to all types of medical interventions; however, the scope of disclosure was hard to determine when solely based on this article. The RPR adopts a detailed approach to disclosure in terms of its topics, scope and standards (*see also* paragraphs 220 et seq.).

RPR emphasizes that the information should first be given to the patient. However, certain conditions where informing the individual is not necessary to have also been stated in RPR. Accordingly, when the patient is a minor or incompetent, the parent or the legal guardian of the individual should be informed, as stated in the second paragraph of Article 15.

I. The Right to Access Medical Records and Demand Correction

281. Article 16 of RPR recognizes the patient's right to access information and his/her records maintained by the healthcare institution. The patients may access such data directly, or through their lawyers and legal representatives. Article 17 defines the right to demand correction and to object to information in the reports. However, whether the personal notes of the physician can be accessed and whether the right to demand correction applies to the personal notes of the physician have not been addressed in the law.

J. Disclosure in a Comprehensible Manner

282. RPR's provisions in Article 18 emphasize that the information to be given to patients should be clear, easily understandable and free of medical terms when possible. The article also states that the psychological status of the patient receiving the information should also be considered, and the information given should leave no space for doubt or hesitation.

K. Certain Conditions Where Disclosure May Not Be Appropriate

283. Article 19 defines certain situations where withholding information from patients can be appropriate. The Regulation states that if the disclosure of the diagnosis will worsen the patient's emotional and clinical status, then it is possible not to inform the patient. This initiative, known as the therapeutic privilege, is criticized with respect to other patient rights such as the right to self-determination and privacy. The same article also states that if the patient has not previously stated otherwise, information can be disclosed to the relatives of the patient in cases where there is no treatment for the condition. However, the Professional Code of Ethics issued by the Turkish Medical Association indicates that the relatives of the patient can only be informed in cases when the patient refuses to learn the truth. Although the guidelines are not primarily a law text, the difference in the approach of the two documents to the issue is noteworthy.

L. The Right Not to Know

284. RPR recognizes the right to refuse information, or the 'right not to know', as it is commonly referred to. Article 20 states that the patient may demand information to be withheld from himself/herself or his/her family. However, it is also emphasized that this right does not apply to certain conditions where the appropriate measures in accordance with legislations must be taken by the authorities. While RPR does not define these exceptional situations, the most relevant example would be cases of communicable diseases requiring mandatory notification from the health authorities. Thus, it could be argued that RPR limits the so-called right not to know and requires the notification of individuals regardless of their request in such cases.[97]

M. The Right to Privacy

285. RPR's Article 21 includes provisions on the right to privacy in healthcare. The provisions address both the physical privacy of patients and the confidentiality of patient information. The first paragraph of the article includes a general provision on privacy, stating that the right to privacy should be respected during the provision of healthcare services.

The second paragraph includes six separate items aiming to protect the physical privacy of the patients and the confidentiality of patient information.

---

97. G. Sert, Hasta Hakları Uluslararası Bildirgeler ve Tıp Etiği Açısından (*Patient Rights from the Perspective of International Documents and Medical Ethics*) (Babil Yayınları İstanbul, 2004), s. 141.

286. There are different opinions in Turkish legal doctrine regarding the obligation to maintain the confidentiality of personal information after the death of a person.[98] Article 21 mentioned above states that confidentiality should be maintained after death and resolves the debate around this issue, at least partially, for healthcare providers.

287. According to RPR, all sorts of diagnostic and therapeutic interventions and other procedures requiring physical contact are to be performed under appropriate conditions respecting confidentiality, as stated in part (b) of the second paragraph of Article 21. The next paragraph of the same article emphasizes the importance of consent in healthcare institutions with medical training facilities (such as hospitals of faculties of medicine). This last paragraph states that for healthcare professionals other than those directly involved in patient's care to be present during an intervention, the patient's consent must be sought prior to the intervention.

In addition, the second paragraph of Article 21 also states that healthcare service should not interfere with the personal or family life of the individual unless it is necessary.

Article 23 can also be considered to focus on the right to privacy. Accordingly, under conditions when divulging confidential patient information may result in total violation of the personal rights of the patient, the person is liable even if the patient has consented to such an act. The Regulation states that such information can only be divulged under legally and ethically justifiable situations.

N. Obtaining the Consent of the Patient

288. Consent of the patient is emphasized in many other legal documents, including the Constitution of the Turkish Republic. Article 22 of RPR states that the individual cannot be subjected to medical interventions without his/her consent, whereas Article 24 affirms that the consent of the individual is essential prior to any intervention to be performed upon the individual. If the consent has not been obtained in parallel with the provisions related to disclosure, as stated in Articles 15 and 18, then the consent is not valid and thus the intervention will be unlawful. Revisions of PRR in 2014 are as follows:

- PRR's 1998 version requires an interpreter, if necessary, to communicate with the patient. In 2014, revision of PRR emitted this requirement and added the requirements to inform the patient depending on his/her social and cultural status. The procedure of informed consent should be done without suspicion and uncertainty for the comprehension of the patient.
- PRR's 1998 version requires that the information should be given by healthcare personnel who is responsible for medical intervention. However, in 2014, revised version of the Regulation enlarged this personnel. The 2014 version requires

98. Donay, *supra* s. 143.

information to patient as a compulsory act. In case of patient requirement, the information can be given to his/her legal representatives instead of himself/ herself.

289. The Regulation states that for patients without a legally appointed guardian or parent for incompetent individuals, when it is medically required to intervene yet the guardian or the parent does not consent to the procedure, intervention can be performed with a court order sought in line with the relevant provisions defined in Turkish Civil Code. However, in medical emergencies, the intervention may first be initiated and the court order may be sought later.

O. Withdrawing Consent

290. The Regulation states that withdrawing the consent once the treatment has been started is possible on condition that there are no medical drawbacks involved. While such drawbacks are not addressed in the Regulation, this statement can be considered to limit the right to refuse treatment under certain conditions. Within this framework, the right to refuse an already initiated treatment is limited to conditions where no unfavourable medical consequences will occur. Therefore, this provision can be considered to restrict the right to refuse treatment within certain limits (*see also* paragraph 291).

P. The Right to Refuse Treatment

291. RPR's Article 25 defines the right to refuse treatment. The article states that individuals have the right to refuse treatment except in cases mandated by law. Examples of cases where mandatory treatment is required include those stated in the General Health Law (*Umumi Hıfzıssıhha Yasası*). The Regulation also emphasizes the importance of disclosure with regard to the consequences of refusing treatment, as stated in Article 15. PRR's 2014 version emphasizes that unconscious patients' willingness before their unconscious state should be taken into account.

Q. Medical Interventions for Incompetent Individuals

292. According to Article 26 of RPR, the consent of the minor patients, in addition to informed permission of parents, is necessary. However, the provisions of RPR on this issue are still not in accordance with those of Turkish Civil Law, which clearly states that competent minors do not need permission to freely exercise their own rights, which are strictly related to their individual being.

Chapter 2. The Physician–Patient Relationship in Specific Terms

§1. Minor Patients

I. The Legal Status of Minors in Medical Interventions

293. The legal framework regulating the status of minors in medical practice in Turkey includes some controversial provisions that may give rise to problems related to the practice of personal rights, as well as ethically controversial actions. Obtaining the consent of the individual, informing the minor's family, and proxy decision-making by the parent or legal representative may under certain conditions present problems with regard to the personal rights of the minor individual.

II. The Concept of the Minor in Turkish Civil Law

294. According to Article 11 of the Turkish Civil Code, the individual becomes an adult (mature) after he/she has fully completed 18 years of age, and he/she is no longer considered a minor. Thus, the term 'minor' includes everyone younger than 18 years in the Turkish legal system. The United Nations Convention on the Rights of the Child (which has been ratified by Turkey after following its publication in the RG and which now operates as a part of Turkey's national legislation) also states that every human being below the age of 18 years should be considered a child (Article 1).

A. Legal Representative

295. According to the Civil Law's Article 335, minors who are not adults are under the guardianship of their parents. This gives the parents certain rights. One of these rights is the authority to represent, as stated in Article 342 of the Civil Code. Accordingly, representation authority assigned to parents does not need the verdict of a court in order to be used. A legally appointed representative (a custodian) is determined for any minor who is not under the guardianship of a parent.

Civil Code, Article 445, states that the authority granted to the custodian to represent the minor or the restricted individual is the same as the one granted to a guardian.

III. Medical Interventions and Minors

296. In Turkish law, one must have the capacity for discernment (or should be *competent*) and should be above 18 years of age in order to be a party in a contractual relationship. Therefore, a minor (who is below 18 years of age by definition) is not considered to have authority to decide on medical interventions even if he/she has the capacity for discernment. Such conditions require the consent of the legal representative (the custodian or the guardian) in the child's name. This situation does not pose any problems in cases where the minor has an absolute lack of discernment. As a rule, the legal representative's decision must be followed under such conditions.

297. However, the situation is different in the case of minors who can comprehend and appreciate the reasons and consequences of the medical intervention. The RPR states that minors should be included in the decision-making process as much as possible.

A. *Obtaining the Consent of the Minors with Discernment Capacity*

298. Minors who are younger than 18 years of age but have discernment capacity, or persons who are older than 18 years but have been legally restricted by court order, have the right to self-determination but such right has a limited status. Persons in this status, known as 'limited competence' (*sınırlı ehliyetsizlik*) in Turkish law, cannot act on their own in legal processes without the permission or approval of their legal representative (custodian or guardian). However, they may exercise some rights that are strictly related to the individual's personal being without seeking the permission or approval of their legal representative. The physical integrity and health of the individual are among such rights. Therefore, individuals in the limited competence status (minors with discernment capacity, and legally restricted adults, such as those with a mental disease or diminished mental capacity) should be able to act freely regarding decisions on medical interventions interfering with their physical integrity. However, LPOMRA, which is a specific legislation regulating the practice of medicine, necessitates the consent of the custodian or the guardian for medical interventions to be performed on individuals below 18 years of age and does not allow these persons to consent for such interventions on their own.

B. *Disclosure of Information to the Minor*

299. Within the context of the provisions outlined above, when the term 'minor' is understood in the broad sense so as to include all patients below 18 years of age – regardless of their capacity to comprehend and act reasonably – it may cause the violation of other rights for many patients. For instance, because the process of consent requires adequate disclosure of relevant information for the decision-maker, the decision-making process advocated in the legislation (which does not allow minors with the capacity for discernment to use their right to self-determination with regard to medical treatment) would require disclosure of normally confidential information – such as HIV seropositivity – to the parents of an adolescent patient between 14 and 17 years of age. However, such practice would be controversial with regard to the right to privacy.[99]

---

99. G. Sert, Hasta Hakları Uluslararası Bildirgeler ve Tıp Etiği Açısından (*Patient Rights from the Perspective of International Documents and Medical Ethics*) (Babil Yayınları İstanbul, 2004), s. 133.

300. Information should first be disclosed to the minor. However, in some regulations, such as the RPR, certain conditions where it is not necessary to inform the patient himself/herself have been determined. Accordingly, when the patient is a minor, lacks discernment capacity or is restricted by a court order, it is stated that the custodian or the guardian of the patient should be informed (Article 15, paragraph 2). LPOMRA also states that informing the legal representative of the minor in the limited competence category (the minor individual with discernment capacity) is compulsory.

C. Refusal of Medical Intervention for the Minor by the Legal Representative

301. According to Article 24 of Regulation on Patient's Rights, under conditions where it is medically compulsory to intervene but the legal representative does not consent to the procedure for a minor, a court order can be sought and the intervention can then be performed based on this order. The issue has been addressed in Civil Code's Article 346. Accordingly, if the interests and development of the child are endangered and the parents cannot find a solution, or if it is beyond the parents' power to solve the issue, then the court judge should take the necessary precautions. In addition, Article 24 of the RPR states that such court permission is not required in emergency cases where the intervention has to be carried out immediately.

IV. Minors and Organ Transplantation

302. The Law on Organ Transplantation prohibits the procurement of organs and tissues from minors below 18 years of age. The RPR also includes the same provision. Turkey has dissented from Article 20 of the Oviedo Convention, which under strict conditions allows procurement of regenerative tissue from minors.[100] Therefore, procurement of organs or tissues for transplantation from minors is forbidden in Turkish law.

V. Minors and Termination of Pregnancy

303. Termination of pregnancy for minors requires the consent of the legal representative of the minor. However, decisions involving reproduction are also a right strictly related to the personal being of the individual, and allowing minors with limited competence to decide on such issues could be acceptable. Yet, the law states

100. O. Gir, Türk Ceza Yasasının (2004), *Organ Aktarımı ile İlgili Maddelerinin Tıp Etiği Açısından Değerlendirilmesi* (*Evaluation of Organ Transplantation Laws or Related Laws with Regard to Medical Ethics*). MÜ. Sağlık Bilimleri Enstitüsü, Yüksek Lisans Tezi (*Unpublished MSc. Thesis*) (İstanbul, 2006). Danışman: (*Mentor*) Şefik Görkey, s. 81.

that the consent of the minor's legal representative should be sought for interventions related to the termination of pregnancy, as in the case of other medical intervention processes detailed above.[101]

§2. The Mental Patient

304. Turkish laws do not include a specific legislation on mentally incapacitated patients. The status of these individuals with regard to medical interventions is determined by the general provisions in the law.

Individuals with legal capacity (adults with discernment capacity and with no legally imposed restriction) may decide on the medical interventions to be performed on them with their free will. No one else – apart from the exceptions defined by the law – is authorized to make such decisions for the individual. The legal representatives may decide for those lacking discernment capacity. However, while mental disease is one of the conditions that abolishes such capacity, not all psychiatric disorders incapacitate the individual in such manner. Therefore, a mentally ill patient may be considered to have legal capacity in so far as he/she acts reasonably. If the disease is severe enough to abolish discernment capacity, then the legal capacity of the individual may cease to exist. Yet, the mental incompetence referred to by the law implies inadequately developed or undeveloped mental facilities; certain degrees of mental incompetence have not been addressed, and in certain cases of mental diseases, the individual may have the legal capacity to act reasonably. For this reason, concrete aspects should be considered when determining the capacity of the individual in the case of a mental disease.

Individuals lacking discernment may not act on their own in legal processes; they are referred to as totally incompetent individuals. Therefore, they do not have the authority to decide on medical intervention. Instead, their legal representative (custodian or guardian) may decide on their behalf. In other words, such individuals may be subject to medical intervention if their legal representative consents to the procedure. Under certain circumstances, a court order may be necessary in addition to the consent of the representative. For instance, the legislation on abortion necessitates a court order in addition to other requirements.[102] In case there is no legal representative, then a representative is appointed by the court for the individual.

§3. The Dying Patient

305. There is no specific legislation addressing the status of the dying patient in Turkish law. However, the RPR, MDR and the Professional Code of Ethics of TPA have provisions dealing with the subject.

---

101. M. Çokar, *Dünyada ve Türkiye'de İsteyerek Düşüğün Yasal Boyutunun Etik Aştdan Değerlendirilmesi (Ethical Evaluation of the Legal Aspect of Voluntary Abortion in Turkey and in the World).* Marmara Üniversitesi Sağlık Bilimleri Enstitüsü, Doktora Tezi *(Ph.D. Thesis, soon to be published)* (İstanbul, 2006). Danışman: *(Mentor)* Şefik Görkey, s. 233.
102. Çokar, *supra* para. 249, n. 1, ss 232–233.

306. Article 14 of MDR states that the physician is under the obligation to protect the life and health of the patients. In cases where it may not be possible to do so, the physician has the duty to relieve the pain of the individual or take the necessary precautions to ameliorate the suffering of the individual. A similar provision has been included in Article 14 of RPR. Furthermore, the Professional Code of Ethics of TPA, Article 28, also states that terminally ill patients should be provided with all sorts of humane care and their suffering should be alleviated as much as possible.

I. Refusal of Treatment

307. Article 25 of PRR 1998 recognizes the right to refuse treatment for patients. However, it has been stated in this article that the patient has the right to refuse treatment except in cases where intervention is legally compulsory. In addition, Article 24 of the RPR states that a patient can withdraw his/her consent for an already initiated intervention on the condition that no medical drawbacks exist for such an action. Therefore, the right to refuse treatment has been defined in somewhat narrowed limits in Turkish law. It should, however, be noted that there are different opinions regarding this right in Turkish legal doctrine. The right to refuse treatment is addressed in a broader context by some, defending that treatment cannot be continued against the patient's refusal.[103] By contrast, another author suggests that Article 24 of the RPR mentioned above is a barrier for such a broad definition. Accordingly, if clear and irreversible harm is to occur regarding a patient's health or life when an acute intervention is discontinued, then the patient cannot withdraw his/her consent.[104,105] The difference between Articles 24 and 25 is also noteworthy. These two articles suggest that a physician will not be liable if he/she respects the choice of the patient and does not initiate a treatment in case of treatment refusal; however, if the physician, in accordance with the patient's demand, stops treatment after it has been initiated, then he/she will be liable. This controversial situation has also been criticized, and the difference implied in the provision regarding these two acts has been found meaningless.[106]

II. Withholding Treatment

308. There are no provisions on withholding treatment support; however, it should be noted once again that Turkish law imposes upon the physician the obligation to take the necessary precautions for the protection of the patient's life. Do Not Resuscitate (DNR) codes have currently not been addressed in Turkish law.

103. Hakeri, *supra* para. 96, n. 2, s. 240.
104. Erman, *supra* para. 177, n. 2, s. 170.
105. G. Sert, Hasta Hakları Uluslararası Bildirgeler ve Tıp Etiği Açısından (*Patient Rights from the Perspective of International Documents and Medical Ethics*) (Babil Yayınları İstanbul, 2004), s. 155.
106. Inceoğlu, *supra* para. 104, n. 3, s. 78.

Chapter 3. Specific Activities

§1. (Induced) Abortion

I. Historical Overview

309. The development of legislations on abortion can be examined in two phases: Ottoman Era and Turkish Republic period.

A. *Ottoman Era*

310. Before 1858, abortion procedures were punished according to Islamic religion provisions *(şeriat)*. These provisions imposed community service and money fine (to be paid to the family of the woman) for those who performed an induced abortion.

311. Ceza Kanunname-i Hümayunu, enacted in 1858, included provisions on induced abortion in its Articles 192–193.[107] These articles defined induced abortion as a criminal offence, performed either with or without the consent of the woman. Providing the devices or drugs required to induce abortion was also defined as a criminal offence. The same articles also impose sanction for the woman willingly inducing the abortion of her own child. Commission of the criminal offences described in these articles by healthcare workers required increased sanction.

B. *Development of Induced Abortion Procedures in the Laws of the Turkish Republic*

312. Induced abortion was not a legal procedure in the Turkish Republic until 1965. With the realization of unfavourable consequences of illegally induced abortion attempts which threatened public health, induced abortion was legalized and its limits were defined.[108]

313. There are two main laws on induced abortion in Turkey. The first law, issued on 27 May 1983 in the Official Journal, is called 'Law on Population Planning' *(Nüfus Planlaması Hakkında Kanun)*. This law is also supported by several other legislations, including 'Regulation on the Education, Duties, Authorization and Responsibilities of the Personnel Performing Population Planning Services' *(Nüfus Planlaması Hizmetlerini Yürütecek Personelin Eğitimi, Görev, Yetki ve Sorumlulukları Hakkında Yönetmelik)* issued on 10 September 1983; 'Regulation on the Practice of Population Planning Services' *(Nüfus Planlaması Hizmetlerini Yürütme Yönetmeliği)* issued on 6 October 1983 and Regulation No. 510, which is

107. E. Yurtcan, *Türk Hukukunda Kürtaj ve Uygulaması (Therapeutic Abortion in Turkish Law and Its Application)*. 2. bası, Kazancı Kitap Ticaret A.Ş. (İstanbul 1990), ss 30–33.
108. E. Yurtcan, *ibid.*, ss 20–26.

also called 'Regulation on the Practice and Inspection of Abortion and Sterilization Services' (*Rahim Tahliyesi ve Sterilizasyon Hizmetlerinin Yürütülmesi ve Denetlenmesine İlişkin Tüzük*) issued on 18 November 1983.

314. The second law, which addresses induced abortion in terms of criminal law, is the Turkish Penal Code. Articles on induced abortion have been in existence in Turkish criminal law starting from the Penal Law adopted from the French Penal Code and issued in 1858 during the Ottoman Empire era. Following the foundation of the Turkish Republic, similar articles were also included in the Turkish Penal Code enacted in 1926. Induced abortion as a criminal offence was addressed in this Code in Articles 468–471. The regulations on this issue have been amended four times, including the changes made in Law on Population Planning (*Nüfus Planlaması Hakkında Kanun*), No. 2827, issued in 1965. Finally, the whole Turkish Penal Code was changed and criminal offences with regard to induced abortion were last defined in Articles 99 and 100 of the new Code.

315. The purpose of Law on Population Planning (*Nüfus Planlaması Hakkında Kanun*), No. 2827, as stated in its Article 1, is to define the principles of population planning and to regulate the issues regarding induced abortion, sterilization interventions, emergency situations requiring immediate intervention and the supply, manufacture and determination of drugs and devices for prevention of pregnancy. Article 2 of the law defines population planning with the following statement: 'Population planning refers to parents being able to have children in the desired number and at the desired time.' The last sentence of the second paragraph of the same article states that population planning is to be achieved by means of measures that will prevent pregnancy. Thus, the law uses population planning, contraception and family planning synonymously.

Addressing induced abortion and family planning within the scope of the same law was met with criticism at first; however, considering the relation of the issue with family planning, it could be concluded that addressing the two issues at the same time was actually an appropriate approach.

II. Conditions for Performing Induced Abortions

316. The most important amendment in the law is the one addressing the termination of pregnancy in Article 5 of the Regulation on the Practice and Inspection of Abortion and Sterilization Services. According to the article, dilatation and curettage of the uterus can be performed on demand until the completion of the tenth week of the pregnancy if the mother's health status allows the procedure.

A. Time Constraints

317. The duration of pregnancy is calculated by physicians and other healthcare workers by using the date of last menstruation, which is approximately two weeks later than the moment of conception and at least three weeks later than the time of implantation. Since no clear method for detection of the starting time of pregnancy has been provided in the legislation, the duration calculated for medical pregnancy is used in practice by healthcare professionals.

B. The Situation in Pregnancies Longer Than Ten Weeks

318. When the duration of pregnancy has exceeded ten weeks, the procedure can only be performed if the pregnancy is threatening or will threaten the mother's life, or if the child's birth will cause serious harm for the child and for the generations that will follow. Such intervention has to be based on objective findings based on reports prepared by an obstetrician and by another physician specializing in the relevant field of medicine.

319. It should also be noted that medical emergencies constitute an exception and the time limit does not apply under such conditions. In Article 7 of the Regulation on the Practice and Control of Abortion and Sterilization Services and Article 5 of Law on Population Planning, the physician in charge is authorized to intervene and perform induced abortion when such an 'emergency that threatens life or one of the vital organs' is present. However, according to the law, this emergency intervention can only be performed by a gynaecology and obstetrics specialist. In addition, according to Article 9 of the same legislation, the physician has to notify the relevant health management authority of the state (Provincial Health Directorates in provinces and State Physician in the county) before the intervention, if possible, or within twenty-four hours following the intervention.

C. Consent for Induced Abortion

320. The Law on Population Planning *(Nüfus Planlaması Hakkında Kanun)*, No. 2827, addresses the issue of consent in Article 6.

1. Consent of the Pregnant Woman

321. In induced abortion procedures, the consent of the pregnant woman is required, as defined in both Law on Population Planning and Turkish Penal Code. It is essential that the woman demanding the procedure acts on her free will. In the presence of reasons that eliminate free will, consent cannot be valid. In addition, Regulation on the Practice and Control of Abortion and Sterilization Services includes a sample consent form, which suggests that consent for this procedure has to be obtained in written form.[109]

---

109. For a detailed review of this Regulation from the perspective of Turkish legal doctrine and medical ethics, *see* S. Duran, G. Sert & Ş. Görkey, *Rahim Tahliyesi ve Sterilizasyon Hizmetlerinin Yürütülmesi ve Denetlenmesine İlişkin Tüzük'ün Aydınlatılmış Onam ile İlgili Hükümlerinin Tıp Etiği ve Tıp Hukuku Açısından Değerlendirilmesi (Review of the Provisions of Regulation on the Practice and*

322. Article 14 of Regulation on the Practice and Control of Therapeutic Abortion and Sterilization Services states that consent will not be sought in cases where the patient lacks the competence to consent due to mental disease. Even if consent has been given, such consent cannot be considered valid. The conditions under which the pregnancy of such a woman can be terminated are not clear in the law. Whether induced abortion can be performed on a woman that lacks competence due to a mental disorder is an ethically controversial issue that is not addressed in the Turkish legislations. The legal procedure to be followed is clear if the woman is under custody. In such cases, the consent of the legally appointed representative and the approval of the court must be sought. However, if the woman that lacks competence to consent due to a mental disease is not under custody, this issue is a problematic one that is not covered in the law.[110] It should be noted that the relevant provisions on medical emergencies will apply under such circumstances.

2. Consent of the Minor and Permission of the Parents

323. For minors to utilize induced abortion services, the consent of the minor and the permission of her parents are required. A physician inducing an abortion with the consent of the minor but without the permission of the parent can be subject to criminal sanction for violating the provisions laid out in the Law on Population Planning. If the physician committing the act is employed in the private sector, a monetary fine is imposed, whereas, for state-sector physicians, disciplinary sanction is applied.

324. In situations where induced abortion is performed without the consent of the minor, the criminal offence committed is defined as 'induced abortion without consent'.

3. Approval of the Parent and of the Court Judge

325. For incompetent persons under custody, in addition to the permission of the parent, the approval of a court judge is also required by the law for induced abortion procedures. If the consent of the individual has not been obtained, the criminal offence committed is again defined under the title of 'induced abortion without consent'. If induced abortion has been performed solely on the consent of the person under custody, but the guardian's and/or the judge's approval has not been sought,

---

Control of Therapeutic Abortion and Sterilization about Informed Consent with Regard to Medical Law and Medical Ethics). IV. Lokman Hekim Tıp Tarihi ve Folklorik Tıp Günleri Manisa-Bergama 10–13 Mayıs 2005. Kongre Bildiri Özetleri Kitabı s. 38; Ş. Görkey, Gebeliğin Sonlandırılmasında Karşılaşılan Etik Sorunlar (*Ethical Issues Encountered During the Termination of Pregnancy*). Ed: Hatemi, H., Doğan Yüce, H., Medikal Etik (Doğum, Ölüm Süreçleri ve Yaşamın Anlamı). Reklam Yayım Dağıtım, A.Ş. (İstanbul 2001), ss 80–109.

110. Çokar, *supra* para. 249, n. 1, ss 232–234.

this constitutes a criminal offence. If the physician committing the act is employed in the private sector, a monetary fine is imposed, whereas, for state-sector physicians, disciplinary sanction is applied.

4. The Spouse's Permission

326. When the pregnant woman is married, the Law on Population Planning requires the spouse's permission in addition to the woman's consent prior to induced abortion.

5. Informed Consent Procedures

327. The importance of consent for induced abortion is emphasized in several regulations. The Regulation on the Practice and Control of Therapeutic Abortion and Sterilization Services also includes a sample consent form.

III. Induced Abortion in the Turkish Penal Code

328. Criminal offences and corresponding sanctions with regard to induced abortion have been defined in the Turkish Penal Code. The new Turkish Penal Code, dated 26 September 2004, includes provisions on induced abortion in its Articles 99 and 100.

329. According to the Turkish Penal Code mentioned above, if the consent of the individual has been obtained for the procedure, then the duration of pregnancy is the most important factor for determining whether a criminal offence has been committed. If the duration of pregnancy does not exceed ten weeks, then induced abortion performed with the consent of the individual is not considered a criminal offence. Procedures performed within the tenth week do not constitute a criminal offence either since the law uses the term 'more than 10 weeks'. If the duration of the pregnancy does not exceed ten weeks, self-induced abortion by the individual is also not a criminal act, regardless of the device used for the act.

If the termination of pregnancy whose duration has not exceeded ten weeks has been performed with the consent of the individual by an authorized person, this act does not constitute a criminal offence. According to the Regulation on the Practice and Control of Therapeutic Abortion and Sterilization Services, persons authorized to perform termination of pregnancy are gynaecology and obstetrics specialists. In addition, certified general practitioners can terminate pregnancy by using the menstrual regulation method, but such intervention requires the supervision of an obstetrics-gynaecology specialist. However, if the physician is not certified for the procedure, then the procedure constitutes a criminal offence even if the duration of pregnancy does not exceed ten weeks.

The law proposes criminal sanction for persons performing induced abortion with the consent of the individual in pregnancies exceeding ten weeks. This person may or may not be authorized to perform the procedure. If the authorized person is performing the procedure in the presence of medical indications, then no criminal offence is present. If the individual committing this act is not an authorized person, then an increase in the sanction will be in effect.

A pregnant woman willingly aborting a pregnancy exceeding ten weeks constitutes a criminal offence.

If the woman has not consented to induced abortion, performing the procedure constitutes a criminal offence regardless of the duration of pregnancy. In pregnancies not exceeding ten weeks, if induced abortion is performed by an authorized person, then the only criterion for determining whether a criminal offence has been committed is the presence of (or lack of) consent.

According to the Turkish Penal Code, termination of a pregnancy resulting from an offence where the woman is the victim can be performed on condition that the duration of pregnancy does not exceed twenty weeks and the woman's consent has been obtained. However, under such conditions, pregnancy has to be terminated by specialists in a hospital. The relevant articles of the Turkish Penal Code propose increased sanction when the woman dies or suffers physical or psychological harm as a result of the act. In a similar fashion, unauthorized persons causing this harm are also subject to increased penal sanction.

§2. Sterilization

330. Development of legislations on sterilization procedures in Turkey was parallel to those of abortion. Sterilization interventions were forbidden during the early years of the Turkish Republic. In the following decades, it was determined that sterilization could be used in medical emergencies (1965). With the changes made in 1985, the procedures became legal on the condition that it is performed at the demand of the person.

331. Sterilization procedures are regulated by the Law on Population Planning, issued in 1983. The Regulation on the Practice and Inspection of Abortion and Sterilization Services, a secondary law issued in line with the Law on Population Planning, also includes provisions on sterilization interventions.

332. The Law on Population Planning, Article 2, states that sterilization services will be controlled and monitored by the state. The definition of sterilization is given as 'the cessation of the ability of a woman or a man to have a child without affecting the ability of the individual to have sexual intercourse'. According to the same article, as long as there is no medical contraindication, sterilization can be performed when an adult requests it.

The Law on Population Planning, Article 6, states that for married individuals to undergo sterilization, both the individual and his or her spouse should consent to the procedure.

333. The new Turkish Penal Code (2004) addresses the issue under the title of sterilization in its Article 101. Accordingly, performing sterilization on an individual without the consent of the individual is a criminal offence. The criminal sanction to be imposed is defined as three to nine years of imprisonment. If the act is performed by a person unauthorized to perform the intervention, increased penal sanction is required.

334. There is no specific legislation regulating castration procedures in Turkish law. However, the Law on Population Planning, Article 4, allows the performance of castration during the course of a surgical intervention if the castration is medically required. This provision, which allows castration of the individual without seeking consent, is being criticized. Some authors have pointed out the need for a specific regulation on castration and emphasized the importance of informed consent for the issue.[111]

§3. Assisted Reproduction

335. In Turkish law, ART services are regulated with the Regulation on Health Care for Assisted Reproduction Treatment *(Üremeye Yardımcı Tedavi (ÜYTE) Merkezleri Yönetmeliği)* (RHCART). The Regulation was issued in 1987, but it has been amended several times afterwards.

A new 'Regulation on Assisted Reproduction Procedures and Assisted Reproduction Centres' (*Üremeye Yardımcı Tedavi Uygulamaları ve Üremeye Yardımcı Tedavi Merkezleri Hakkında Yönetmelik*) (RARPAPR) has been issued (published in the Official Journal of Turkish Republic on 6 March 2010) by the Ministry of Health. On 30 September 2014, the above-mentioned regulation was abolished again, and a new regulation came into force with the same title (*Üremeye Yardımcı Tedavi Uygulamaları ve Üremeye Yardımcı Tedavi Merkezleri Hakkında Yönetmelik*).

In 2018, a law was added to the LOT with regard to ART. Since then, important provisions of the law relating to ART-level applications in Turkey have been connected in LOT. According to the additional Article 1 added to the LOT, the provisions brought by the article provided for the regulation of the general issues regulated by the law. The article states that in cases where there is no natural childbearing or medical necessity, the reproductive cells or embryo can be transferred to the expectant mother by fertilizing the male and/or male reproductive cells by medical means and fertilizing them inside or outside the body. According to the above-mentioned article, these practices can only be applied between married spouses. According to the same article, these treatments can be performed only by physicians authorized by the Ministry of Health and within the reproductive-assisted treatment centres licensed by the Ministry of Health within the framework of the medical principles determined by the Ministry of Health. In the supplement, reproductive cells from one or both spouses and the embryo derived from these cells are prohibited from being administered to other persons and surrogate motherhood (additional Article 1/2). In addition, donation by the use of another reproductive cell

111. Ayan, *supra* para. 45, n. 1, s. 28.

and/or embryo, and donation, sale, possession, use, storage, transportation, import, export and intermediation of the reproductive cell and/or embryo for this purpose are prohibited (additional Article 1/3).

Utilization of Reproductive Techniques Services Within the Scope of GHI

The GHI Law provides individuals with the right to benefit from reproductive techniques services in order to have children or to receive treatment within the scope of GHI provided that they meet certain conditions (Article 63/e) (Law Amending Certain Health-Related Laws and Decree Laws. Law No. 7151, RG: 5.12.2018 revised this provision). According to this regulation, certain conditions are required for the insured patients to benefit from these services:

(1) Couples should be married.
(2) It should be medically documented that couples cannot have children naturally by applying normal medical treatments.
(3) The woman should be at least 23 years old and under 40 years old.
(4) One of the spouses should have GHI for at least five years.
(5) The medical committee has documented that other treatment methods have failed in the last three years, except in cases of primary ovarian failure of the woman and azoospermia of the man. In that case, the couple has a right to try treatment a maximum of three times.

In the same amendment, persons with hereditary diseases or carriers are entitled to benefit from these rights. Accordingly, couples with hereditary diseases or carriers determined by the institution can benefit from these rights in case of being married and insured. If the treatment of a disease is not possible by any other medical method and is considered medically necessary by the medical committee, the insured spouses can benefit from assisted reproductive treatment.

The above-mentioned medical committee reports should be obtained from the bodies authorized by Social Security Institution.

I. Definition

336. Article 4 of the RARPAPR defines ART as procedures that facilitate the fertilization of the egg of the future mother with the sperm of the husband. These procedures are considered to be applications that have been accepted as a form of treatment in modern medicine and may include the fertilization of the egg outside the human body, as well as the transfer of the gametes or embryos to the reproductive system of the future mother.

II. Aim and Scope

337. According to Article 1 of the Regulation, the aim of RARPAPR is to determine the essential requirements that should be met during the ART procedures that intend to help married couples – who are deemed medically suitable for ART procedures – conceive. The same article also states that the standards that should be met by the ART centres and the inspection procedures of such centres will also be determined by this Regulation.

Article 1 clearly states that the use of ART procedures shall be allowed only for married couples in Turkey and only their own gametes can be used.

338. Article 2 of the Regulation states that RARPAPR applies to public and private institutions, legal and natural persons and regulates their activities concerning ART procedures.

III. Establishment and Inspection of ART Centres and Their Responsibilities

339. Articles 7–9 of the new Regulation state that ART centres, in line with the planning of Ministry of Health, can be established within public and private hospitals where obstetrics-gynaecology departments and adult and newborn intensive care units exist. Article 8's emphasis is on using their own medical staff in both private hospitals and medical centres.

340. Articles 5 and 6 of the Regulation include provisions on the assessment of yearly data, specification of follow-up and evaluation procedures for pregnant women and foetuses induced with ART, determination of the standards of ART and the establishment of a commission, which will provide opinions on the implementation measures of the RARPAPR's provisions.

Article 19 of the Regulation addresses the responsibilities of ART centres; additionally new responsibilities are attached to the previous ones. Accordingly, the centres are responsible for the follow-up of the pregnant women until delivery takes place. These patients need to be monitored by the physicians of the hospitals within which the ART centre is located, and healthcare services for the adult and newborn should be provided if necessary. If the pregnant woman is living in another city, then her follow-up services should be provided by a hospital in that city. Similarly, the woman should be provided with medical care during the delivery process, and other healthcare services for the newborn and the mother should be provided by that hospital if necessary. Women who failed to follow-up in the process should immediately be reported to the local health administration authority (*İl Sağlık Müdürlüğü*).

New responsibilities are as follows: Independent ART centres should not take responsibility for giving birth. They are only authorized to register and report to responsible authorities.

In case of closing of the ART centres, the Ministry of Health should be informed about the frozen embryos, gonads and cells. The Ministry of Health Representatives are responsible for transferring the frozen embryos and the above-mentioned tissues to the nearest centre.

Another responsibility assigned to the centres concern providing the data on services to the Ministry of Health. The centres are required to provide the list of pregnancies in the previous year at the beginning of every year in January. Furthermore, the centres have an obligation to maintain the forms and documents defined in the Regulation for thirty years.

IV. Personnel Working in ART Centres

341. Article 17 covers the specifications of the personnel who should be employed in ART centres. Accordingly, the responsible manager of the centre is the director or the responsible manager of the hospital in which the ART centre is located. The chief of the ART centre must be an obstetrics and gynaecology specialist certified by the Ministry of Health. The specifications for the person in charge of the ART laboratory differ from those defined in the previous regulation. Accordingly:

- a physician with adequate (at least six months) applied training on reproductive medicine, infertility and assisted reproduction techniques in a training centre in Turkey determined by the Ministry of Health (or in a foreign country);
- a physician, a veterinary, a biologist, a pharmacist or a nurse with a master of science or doctoral degree on assisted reproduction; or
- a histology and embryology specialist with documented training on reproductive medicine, infertility and assisted reproduction techniques may become ART laboratory chief if he/she completes a minimum three-month course on microinjection and andrology laboratory procedures in a training centre in Turkey (or in a foreign country) determined by the Ministry of Health.

In addition, a urologist, an obstetrics-gynaecology specialist and an anaesthesiologist must also be employed within the facility. Furthermore, at least one nurse, one receptionist and an adequate number of cleaning and security personnel must be employed in the centre.

Article 17 of the Regulation states that training courses for working in ART centres may be conducted by centres specified by the Ministry of Health and a separate regulation will be issued on this topic.

V. Prohibitions

342. Article 27 defines a number of prohibitions which do not essentially differ from the previous regulation. However, there are new limits placed on embryo transfer, which aim to prevent unwanted (multiple) pregnancies.

In section 1, the article states that ART procedures that do not meet the requirements specified in the Regulation cannot be performed. Appendix 17 refers to 'contact bureaus' which aim to direct patients to ART centres. It is stated that if the existence of such bureaus (which may belong either to the ART centre owner or to other third parties) is determined, their activities shall be stopped immediately, and centres utilizing these bureaus are to be closed down for thirty days. In addition, section 3 prohibits persons without a work permit from taking part in ART procedures.

Section 4 in Article 18 prohibits the possession, use, transfer and sale of ovum and sperm obtained from couples and embryos produced from these reproductive cells for purposes other than those specified in the Regulation.

Section 5 of Article 18 states that for couples undergoing ART treatment, only their own gametes may be used. Use of gametes of other people who are not candidates, as well as their possession, use, transfer and sale for purposes other than those listed in this Regulation is forbidden. The centres are also prohibited from directing their patients to other local or foreign centres, as emphasized in section 6 of the same article. Section 7 notes that centres acting against the provisions outlined in sections 4–6 of Article 18 are to be notified to the district attorney.

Within this framework, sperm and ovum obtained in ART centres in Turkey can only be used for married couples to whom those reproductive cells belong. Therefore, sperm or ova taken from such couples cannot be used to initiate pregnancy in some other individual and selling these cells to other persons or centres is also prohibited. In addition, use of the sperm or the ovum or embryos formed from such reproductive cells for research purposes is also forbidden.

Section 8 of Article 18 addresses the problem of multiple pregnancies, an unwanted consequence of ART procedures. In order to avoid this consequence, certain prohibitions have been defined. For this purpose, the centres are advised to aim for the development of not more than two follicles during the classic ovulation induction method. If three or more follicles develop during the process, utilizing artificial insemination is prohibited.

In the previous regulation, transfer of up to three embryos was allowed. Transfer of more than three embryos was possible on condition that the physician in charge could document the medical factors (such as age, embryo quality and other similar factors) necessitating such transfer. The new Regulation, in section 8/b of its Article 18, emphasizes that single embryo transfer is essential. The same section also defines the exceptions to this rule. Accordingly, for patients up to 35 years of age, a single embryo may be transferred in the first and the second attempts. However, two embryos may be transferred in the third attempt. Transfer of two embryos is allowed in all patients over 35 years of age. Centres violating these provisions will be subject to certain sanctions. If in the first and the second time a violation is detected, the centre will not be allowed to admit new patients for three and six months, respectively. When such violation occurs for the third time, the centre's licence and the certificate of the ART centre's director will be cancelled.

An important prohibition has been defined in section 9 of Article 19. This section states that, except in situations where sex selection may prevent a serious disorder in the foetus, gonad and/or embryo selection and transfer may not be performed for selecting the gender of the future child.

The Regulation also forbids embryonic or foetal reduction in multiple pregnancies. However, reduction may be performed on condition that the medical indication for reduction has been documented by a report that will be obtained from a university or state hospital. If reduction is performed without documenting the medical indication in the manner described above, sanctions similar to those defined for embryo transfer will also apply in this situation (the above-mentioned prohibitions have been totally moved to Appendix 17 in the new regulation (2014)).

Storage of reproductive cells and gonad tissues has been prohibited in the Regulation. However, certain exceptions to this rule have been defined. Accordingly, such storage is possible in cases of medical necessity.

For male patients, such necessity applies to the situations listed below:

- if the sperm has been obtained with the help of surgical intervention;
- prior to interventions such as radiotherapy and chemotherapy, which may damage the gonads;
- prior to interventions that may result in the loss of reproductive ability;
- if the sperm count is very low.

For female patients, the exceptions include the following:

- prior to interventions such as radiotherapy and chemotherapy which may damage the gonads;
- prior to interventions that may result in the loss of reproductive ability;
- if the woman has no child, has a possibility of early menopause and this situation is confirmed by three specialist physicians (2014).

In order to provide the security of the material, storage of reproductive cells and gonad tissues is to be performed along with a DNA analysis report of the candidate. For situations where such storage is necessary due to very low amount of sperm in males, DNA analysis is not required if the storage period does not exceed ninety days. For longer storage periods, DNA analysis will be required. When this period exceeds one year, the individual should consult the centre and provide his/her written consent if storage of the material is to be continued.

If the owner of the frozen reproductive cells and gonad tissues does not renew the yearly protocol or wishes to terminate the protocol, or if he/she dies, then the material must be destroyed and a written documentation of the procedure must be provided. Section 11 of Article 19 states that, if an electronic database of the Ministry of Health has been established, then information on frozen reproductive cells and gonad tissues is to be recorded in this database.

Section 12 of the same article addresses the issue in question for embryos of couples. In case there are surplus embryos remaining, they can be maintained in frozen form on condition that both partners consent to the procedure. When the storage period exceeds one year, couples should provide written documentation of their ongoing demand for storage and this has to be renewed every year. If the time limit expires, or if one of the spouses dies, or if the couple wants to terminate the storage process or if the couple is officially divorced, then the material must be destroyed and a written documentation of the procedure must be provided. If an electronic database of the Ministry of Health has been established, then information on frozen reproductive cells and gonad tissues is to be recorded in this database.

Article 18 also states that frozen reproductive tissues and gonads can be stored for a maximum of five years.

In addition, the Regulation prohibits all types of advertising activities, including those aiming to provide information about ART procedures and other activities that are not within the scope of the Regulation. The new Regulation gives more detail about the prohibition as follows: Article 24 emphasizes on prohibition of misguiding information and prohibits giving any statistical information apart from scientific publications with the permission of the Ministry of Health.

VI. Consent

343. Article 15 on patient records repeats the requirement for the existence of the marriage bond between couples requesting ART. The same article also emphasizes the importance of written consent forms that must be used for these procedures. The article also defines all the procedures that must be carried out and the information that should be recorded, including the photographs, identification documents and marriage licence copies of the couples.

VII. Administrative Sanctions

344. When centres are determined to have violated the conditions outlined in the Regulation, they may be temporarily closed down, or their licence may be cancelled.

§4. Organ Transplants

I. Historical Background

345. The legislation regulating organ and tissue transplantation procedures entered into force in 1979.[112] Following the recommendation by the Council of Europe in 1978 for the harmonization of the Member State legislations with regard to the removal and transplantation of human biological substances, LOT was issued in 1979. Entering into force right after the recommendation, the law's content and scope were highly influenced by the recommendation.[113] LOT is based on an

112. For a detailed historical review of the process and its early reflections in medical practice in Turkey, *see* M. Haberal et al., *Transplantation Legislation and Practice in Turkey: A Brief History*. 30 Transplantation Procs. 3644–3646 (1998).

113. Ş. Görkey, *Bazı Ülkelerin Organ Aktarımı ile İlgili Yasalarının Aydınlatılmış Onam Açısından Değerlendirilmesi (Evaluation of the Laws on Organ Transplantation of Some Countries with Regard to Informed Consent).* Tıbbi Etik Yıllığı V. II. Tıbbi Etik Sempozyumuna Sunulan Bilgiler. 16 Mar. 1995. Ed. A. Terzioğlu. ss 33–56; Ş. Görkey, G. Baysoy & T. Başkan, *Avrupa Konseyinin Üye Ülkelerinin Organ ve Doku Aktarımı Ile İlgili Yasaları Arasında Uyum Sağlamaya Yönelik Önergesinin Türkiye'deki Organ Aktarımı Yasası İle Karşılaştırılması (The Comparison of the European Council's Directive for Harmonization Between International Laws with the Organ Transplantation Law of Turkey),* 8. Ulusal Adli Tıp Günleri 16–20 Ekim 1995 Antalya, Poster Sunuları *(Poster Presentation),* Ed. Kolusayın, Ö., Yavuz, F.

informed consent model for procurement and transplantation of organs and tissues.[114] However, the addition of certain articles in 1982 suggests a move away from this model, especially within the context of the articles added afterwards.

346. Council of Europe's 'Convention for the Protection of Human Rights and Dignity of the Human Being with Regard to the Application of Biology and Medicine: Convention on Human Rights and Biomedicine' was ratified by Turkey and entered into force in 2003. Thus, the Convention became a part of Turkey's internal legislation, in line with Article 90 of the Constitution of the Turkish Republic. The articles of this Convention apply in Turkey; however, it should also be noted that Turkey has dissented from the provisions outlined in Article 20 of the Convention regarding organ and tissue transplantation.

347. The previous Turkish Penal Code, issued in 1926, did not include specific provisions regarding organ and tissue transplantation. The new Turkish Penal Code, issued in 2004, addresses issues such as the unlawful procurement of organs and tissues, and it describes criminal offences such as organ and tissue trade and helping in such trade.

II. The Definition of Organ and Tissue

348. Procedures related to grafting and transplantation of organs for scientific and medical purposes are regulated with LOT, issued in 1979. Article 2 of the law states that the terms 'organ' and 'tissue' imply all kinds of tissues and organs and their components forming the human body. In addition, the second paragraph of Article 2 states that the law does not apply to autografts, taking and transplantation of hair and skin and blood transfusion procedures.

III. Prohibition of Profit-Based Transplantation

349. Article 3 of LOT prohibits buying and selling of organs and tissues in exchange for a price or any other profit. Turkish Penal Code, issued in 2004, defines purchasing and selling of organs and tissues and negotiating for such acts as a criminal offence.

IV. Advertisement Ban

350. Article 4 of LOT allows spreading of statistical and scientific data and news with regard to organ and tissue transplantation. However, the same article prohibits giving and publishing advertisements about tissue and organ transplantation. The

114. M.E. Sarıal, *Sağlararası Organ Nakillerinden Doğan Hukuksal İlişkiler (Legal Relations Arising from Organ Transplantations Between Living Persons)* (İstanbul, 1986), ss 55–67.

sixth paragraph of Article 91 of the Turkish Penal Code prohibits advertisements regarding the procurement of tissues and organs for any kind of benefit.

V. Procurement of Organs from Living Donors

351. The second part of LOT regulates the procurement of organs and tissues from living donors. Accordingly, procurement of organs and tissues from incompetent individuals under 18 years of age is forbidden. In other words, for a person to be able to donate an organ or a tissue, he/she has to be a competent individual and over 18 years of age, as stated in Article 5 of LOT.

352. According to an additional article to LOT, organ transplantation from living donors can be carried out on relatives up to the fourth degree (including fourth degree). Living donor transplantation between the spouses can be realized when the recipient has been married for at least two years. It is stated in the article that spouses shall not be required to be married for at least two years in cases where the disease requiring transplantation is diagnosed after marriage. According to the same article, it is necessary to apply to the ethics committee for the ethical evaluation of the organ and tissue transfers from living donors to be made persons except abovementioned patients. Applications for this matter should be done to the Organ Transplant Evaluation Ethics Committees established in the province where the organ transfer application is made. Organ Transplant Assessment Ethics Committees are established in each province where there are hospitals providing organ transplantation services. The Commission shall convene at the latest within fifteen days from the date of the application, and in case of emergency, shall convene immediately and take decisions by majority vote. In order to evaluate the objections against the decisions of these commissions, it is stated that the National Organ Transplant Ethics Committee will be formed. The Ethics Committee of the National Organ Transplantation examines, approves, annuls or replaces the Commission by reviewing the decisions of the Commission upon appeal. The decisions of the Ethics Committee of the National Organ Transplantation are accurate. According to the article, the meetings of the commissions and boards shall be held in the form of secret sessions. Information and documents regarding the decisions taken at the meeting are confidential to third parties.

In order to obtain an organ or a tissue from a competent living donor above 18 years of age, a consent form signed with free will by the person himself/herself has to be approved by the physician. Accordingly, the form to be approved by the physician should be signed by the donor in the presence of two witnesses. The donor may also orally state his/her consent and sign the form in the presence of two witnesses. Such a form should also be approved by the physician, as stated in Article 6.

VI. Obligations for Procurement of Organs from Living Donors

353. Article 7 of LOT states certain obligations to be fulfilled by the physicians who will obtain organs from donors. Accordingly, the physician should inform the donor about the risks and medical, psychological, familial and social consequences of organ donation, as stated in paragraph (a). In paragraph (b) of the same article, it is stated that the donor should also be informed about the benefits that will be provided to the recipient. In addition, paragraph (c) of the same article requires physicians to refuse the organ or tissue donation offers of incompetent (due to a mental or psychological condition) individuals.

Article 7 of LOT requires physicians to question whether the married donors' spouses are informed about the procedure and document this with a signed form. This provision suggests that the consent of married individuals' spouses should also be sought prior to donation. Within the framework set by paragraph (d) of Article 7, the potential organ or tissue donor's spouse has to confirm in writing that he/she is aware of the donation and consents to the procedure. However, whether the refusal of the spouse or failure in determination of the marital status of the donor prevents donation is a controversial issue in the legal doctrine.[115] It is assumed that the physician is merely assigned the duty to determine the situation. Thus, it is suggested that there is no legal barrier to perform the procedure. We think that such an issue would be covered under the provisions related to consent if the law aimed to provide such a legal barrier. However, the law provides no information about the way the questioning and determining of the situation should be performed. Situations where the spouse is determined to be informed about the procedure, or where the informed spouse does not consent to procedure, are also unclear and no information is provided. This is in contrast with other parts of the article where there are clear statements regarding the situations when the physician should refuse the donation. Such statements require the refusal of donation offers from incompetent individuals, and donations offered in exchange for any sort of benefit. This suggests that the physician is only assigned the obligation to determine whether the donor's spouse is informed. Turkish legal doctrine suggests that in potentially life-saving donations, determining whether the spouse is informed should be sufficient; however, in donations that are expected to improve the recipient's health, the consent of the donor's spouse should also be sought.[116] The article can be considered to address certain issues physicians should be aware of and handle sensitively.

Article 7 of LOT prohibits the disclosure of the recipient's name, excluding situations where blood or marital relatives or close personal relationships are present. Situations where there is blood or marital relation or a close personal relationship between the donor and the recipient are considered as an exception for medical confidentiality and the identities of the individuals can be disclosed to each other. Any other disclosure performed outside this framework defined by the law may constitute a criminal offence and may be considered an invasion of private life.

115. A. Taşkın, *Organ ve Doku Nakillerinde Hekimin Cezai Sorumluluğu* (*Criminal Liability of the Physician in Organ and Tissue Transplantation*) Adil Yayınevi (Ankara 1997), s. 110.
116. *Ibid.*, s. 110.

VII. Life-Threatening Emergency Situations

354. Article 8 of LOT prohibits the donation of organs or tissues whose removal will absolutely terminate or endanger the life of the donor. Accordingly, only organs or tissues that are considered not essential for the donor can be removed. For this reason, the consent of the individual does not legalize the intervention in such cases. The consent is not valid since it can endanger or terminate the donor's life, even if the donation aims to save another individual's life. Article 24 of the Turkish Civil Code protects personal rights (which also include the right to physical integrity). Within this context, the individual may not consent to unlawful interventions which may harm him/her, and interventions that will absolutely terminate one's life are forbidden.

355. LOT's Article 9 requires the preparation of an approval report after the necessary tests to decrease the risks for the donor's and the recipient's health have been performed. This measure is considered compulsory prior to tissue or organ transplantation procedures and can also be considered to be indirectly related to the provisions outlined in Article 8 above.

VIII. Institutions Where Tissue or Organ Transplantation May Be Performed

356. Article 10 of LOT covers the healthcare institutions authorized to perform organ and tissue transplantation. In this article, expert personnel and institutions possessing the necessary material and equipment are authorized for the interventions. Interventions performed in unauthorized institutions will constitute a criminal offence even if they are carried out successfully. Such acts violate provisions of Article 15 and criminal penalties will be provided in the framework defined in that article. The centres where organ and tissue procedures can be performed and the specifications of such centres are outlined in Regulation for Organ and Tissue Plantation Centres (*Organ ve Doku Nakli Hizmetleri Yönetmeliği*) (ROTTC), issued in 1993.

IX. Procurement of Organs and Tissues from Cadavers

357. As in other countries, the aim in Turkey is also to popularize cadaveric organ and tissue donation. Certain sections of LOT address this issue.

X. Brain Death

358. The third section of LOT addresses issues regarding the cadaveric donation of organs and tissues. Article 11 describes the determination of death. Accordingly, the medical condition of death can be determined by using the guidelines and methods provided by the level of scientific achievements in the country, by the unanimous vote of a group of four physicians consisting of a cardiologist, neurologist, neurosurgeon and anaesthesia and reanimation specialist. The physician treating the recipient and the physician who will remove, transplant or vaccinate the material are prohibited from joining this group, as stated in Article 12. Although Article 11 of the law uses the term 'medical death', the criteria for medical death are not clear. However, the ROTTC, which was issued in 2000, contains an appendix where the criteria for declaration of brain death are defined. In Turkish legal doctrine, it is defended that the criteria of brain death should be used, and the number of physicians needed to declare brain death should be reduced to two.[117] In addition, Article 13 of LOT states that the physicians declaring brain death should note the date, time and cause of death on a form signed by the physicians themselves. The form should be handed to the healthcare institution and maintained by the institution for a duration of ten years.

Furthermore, the appendix of ROTTC mentioned above addresses situations where treatment support may be terminated. Accordingly, following the declaration of brain death, the relatives of the deceased should be notified of the situation. If the relatives decide to donate the organs of the individual, or if the relatives wish to stop the treatment, then treatment support may be terminated.

XI. Organ or Tissue Donation as Indicated in a Will

359. Article 14 of LOT allows the individual to donate his/her whole body or organs or tissues for diagnostic, therapeutic or scientific purposes after his/her death. Accordingly, the individual can also declare this with an official or a written will. In addition, the individual can also state this donation in the presence of two witnesses. According to Turkish Civil Law, an official will can be prepared by a judge, a notary or an authorized state clerk in the presence of two witnesses; whereas a written will, prepared by the individual himself/herself, should contain the place and date (as day, month and year) of the will and should be handwritten and signed by the person. Removal of organs from a living person is possible if the individual is a competent person over 18 years of age. A competent person over 15 years of age can prepare a will and, therefore, can donate organs following his/her death.

XII. Proxy Decisions for Organ and Tissue Donors

360. Under certain circumstances, the relatives of the deceased person can also decide to donate the whole body or organs or tissues of the person. The will of the relatives becomes important in situations where the deceased has not made any statements with regard to the issue while he/she was alive. Accordingly, the consent of the relatives is adequate for the removal of the organs or the tissues of the dead

117. A. Taşkın, *Organ ve Doku Nakillerinde Hekimim Cezai Sorumluluğu* (*Criminal Liability of the Physician in Organ and Tissue Transplantation*) (Ankara: Adil Yayınevi, 1997), s. 123.

person. The law states that the order of priority for the relatives of the person is as follows: the spouse, children over 18 years of age, parents or siblings. The legislation on this issue contains gaps; the procedures to follow in situations where one of the parents or children over 18 years of age does not consent to the procedure have not been determined. Turkish legal doctrine suggests that under such circumstances, the spouse's decision – and if the person has no spouse, then the unanimous decision of the children (over 18 years of age) or parents – should be respected. If none of those relatives exists, then any other relatives' consent can be sought.[118] In Turkish legal doctrine, such relatives can also include persons present during the death of the individual even in the absence of blood or marital relationship. The fiancée, friends or other persons supporting the treatment of the person financially or psychologically can be included within this context.[119]

361. Article 14 of LOT allows the removal of cadaveric organs or tissues without the consent of the deceased or his/her relatives. Unless the person has made a previous declaration to explicitly refuse the procedure or stated such a refusal in his/her will, tissues that are claimed not to affect the physical appearance of the body (such as cornea) can be removed for transplantation purposes without the consent of the relatives.

XIII. Procurement of Organs and Tissue Without Consent

362. LOT was amended in 1982. The amended article allows the removal of tissues or organs from people who died as a result of massive injury caused by a natural disaster or an accident without the consent or will of the individual in case no relatives of the deceased person are near to claim the person's body. In such a situation, it should be declared in a report issued by a committee of physicians that the state of medical death is not due to an injury to the organs planned to be removed and there should be a state of medical emergency threatening the life of the patient awaiting tissue or organ transplantation. This amended article of the law states that an autopsy is to be performed after these procedures, and the report issued by the committee of physicians should be attached to the autopsy report.

XIV. The Status of Unclaimed Cadavers

363. Unclaimed bodies of deceased persons dying in inpatient healthcare institutions and corpses brought to the morgues of such institutions can be donated to

118. A. Taşkın. *Organ ve Doku Nakillerinde Hekimim Cezai Sorumluluğu* (*Criminal Liability of the Physician in Organ and Tissue Transplantation*) (Ankara: Adil Yayınevi, 1997), s. 129.
119. *Ibid.*, s. 130.

higher education institutions after being maintained for six months. For such a donation to take place, there should be no will where the person states otherwise and the corpses should not be related to any criminal investigation.[120]

XV. Criminal Sanctions

364. The next section of LOT covers criminal penalties, as introduced in Article 15. Accordingly, unless more severe criminal sanctions are in force in other laws, the provisions supplied in Article 15 apply to criminal offences violating the provisions of LOT.

365. Article 15 of the LOT was amended in 2018. Penal and administrative sanctions are added to the article. In this article, the sale, purchase and storage of organs, tissues, embryos and reproductive cells against the legislations is prohibited. If the act does not constitute a criminal offence requiring a heavier punishment, three to five years' imprisonment and a judicial fine shall be imposed.

366. In Article 91 of the Turkish Penal Code (2004), removal of an organ from individuals without legally valid consent requires five to nine years of imprisonment, whereas the sanction imposed for removal of a tissue without valid consent is two to five years of imprisonment, as stated in the first paragraph of the relevant article. The valid consent mentioned here should meet the requirements outlined in LOT. If these requirements for consent are not met, this means consent is not valid and requires the criminal sanctions mentioned above.

Unlawful removal of organs or tissues from a cadaver requires imprisonment for up to one year, as stated in the second paragraph of Article 91 of the Turkish Penal Code.

The third paragraph of Article 91 imposes sanctions for individuals purchasing organs or helping in the purchase of organs. Accordingly, such acts require imprisonment between five and nine years. The same paragraph also implies that two to five years of imprisonment will be required for purchasing tissues or helping in the purchase of tissues.

The fourth paragraph of Article 91 states that when removal of organs or tissues without legally valid consent, selling and purchasing of organs or helping in the purchase of organs are committed within an organized crime context, more severe sanctions are to be imposed.

Individuals storing, grafting or transplanting unlawfully obtained organs or tissues are to be sentenced to two to five years of imprisonment, as stated in the fifth paragraph of Article 91.

---

120. T. Akünal, 2238 Sayılı 'Organ ve Doku Alınması, Saklanması ve Nakli Hakkındaki Kanun' *Açısından Hekimin Hukuki Sorumluğu Üzerine Düşünceler (Thoughts on the Civil Liability of the Physician with regard to Law on Procurement, Storage and Transplantation of Organs),* MHAUM Sorumluluk Hukukundaki Yeni Gelişmeler V. Sempozyumu, Türk Hukukunda Hekimin Hukuki ve Cezai Sorumluluğu, 12/13 Mar. 1982, Ankara. ss 19–30.

Individuals advertising, publishing or broadcasting advertisements by any means to obtain an organ or a tissue in exchange for any sort of benefit will be sentenced to one to five years of imprisonment. If death occurs during unlawful removal of organs or tissues from an individual, the relevant sanctions for voluntary manslaughter will apply to persons committing the act.

§5. Experiments on Human Subjects

367. See also paragraph 179.

I. Introduction

368. Research on humans has been addressed in a number of legislations in Turkish law. The 1982 Constitution, in its Article 17, refers to such research and states that 'No one may be subjected to scientific or medical experiments without his or her consent.' This provision is important for two reasons: It emphasizes the importance of consent for research interventions, and it does so at the Constitutional level.

369. MDR (issued in 1960) includes certain provisions in its Articles 10–11 for novel and previously untested methods of diagnosis and treatment; however, the significance of these statements for biomedical research is unclear and they do not provide detailed guidance for biomedical research.

370. Fundamental Law on Health Care Services (*Sağlık Hizmetleri Temel Kanunu*) (issued in 1987) in Article 34 covers the issue of medical research to some extent. The article, in paragraph (k), affirms that:

> the use of previously licensed drugs and preparations on humans for the purpose of scientific research and the production, exporting and selling of drugs that have not been licensed or approved in accordance with the relevant legislation, as well as their use on humans for scientific research, are forbidden when these are performed without the individual's consent and the Ministry of Health's approval.

Thus, the importance of the individual's consent and the Ministry of Health's approval is emphasized for all types of research involving the use of drugs.

II. Regulation on Drug Trials

371. The first RDT, issued in 1993, was prepared to specifically regulate clinical drug trials and should be considered a milestone in Turkish medical law in that respect. However, it is no longer in effect and has historical significance only.

372. In 2008, a new regulation entitled 'RCT' was issued. As the name implies, the new regulation (RCT) had a broader scope and aimed to regulate not only drug trials but also other kinds of clinical research. However, this regulation had to be amended due to a decision by the Supreme Administrative Court, which cancelled a number of provisions in RCT.

373. After a chaotic period regarding the status of research ethics committees and review of clinical research, a new RCT was issued in 2013. *See* paragraph 139.

III. Good Clinical Practice

374. Another noteworthy development in the field of medical research regulations in Turkey was the GCP Guidelines issued by the Ministry of Health in 1995 *(T.C. Sağlık Bakanliği Ilaş ve Eczacılık Genel Müdürlüğü 29 Aralık 1995 Tarihli ve 51748 Sayılı Genelge Eki ve İyi Klinik Uygulamaları Kılavuzu).* These guidelines, in line with the Directive 2001/20/EC, include the definitions of the specific terms for drug trials, GCP principles, protection of research subjects and the requirements for informed consent. Sponsor-researcher monitoring responsibilities, including the insurance of research subjects, are also covered in detail. Thus, the concept of GCP, as outlined in the aforementioned Directive, has been adopted and implemented for clinical drug trials in Turkey.

GCP Guidelines of Turkey was updated a number of times, and the most recent version was issued in April 2013.

IV. Informed Consent

375. As mentioned above, the requirement for the individual's consent for participation in scientific research has been addressed at the Constitutional level in Turkish law.

In addition, protection of the potential research participants and the significance of their consent in clinical research are addressed in a very detailed manner in Articles 5–9 in the second part of RCT (*see also* paragraph 139). Article 5 contains provisions regarding the protection of the volunteers and their informed consent, whereas Articles 6, 7, 8 and 9 refer to research on children, pregnant/breastfeeding women and incompetent individuals, respectively.

Paragraph (ı) of Article 5 of RCT addresses informed consent requirements. Accordingly, potential participants must be informed about the aim and the methods of the study, as well as the expected benefits, foreseen risks and the difficulties involved. In addition, the Regulation requires detailed disclosure regarding the aspects of the study that may be incompatible with the medical condition and the individual characteristics of the volunteer, the conditions under which the study will be carried out, the nature of the data that will be collected and the rationale behind the data collection, as well as the time period the data will be maintained and the rights of the individual as a participant. Paragraph (i) of the same article addresses consent and its documentation. Accordingly, the individual's consent must be documented with an 'informed consent form' and two copies of each form must be available. Paragraph (e) states that the study should be planned so as to minimize pain, discomfort, fear and risks that may arise from the age and the medical condition of the participant. This paragraph also states that these individuals or their legal representatives should be particularly warned when they are included in a clinical study. Paragraph (j) requires the assignment of at least one member of the research team as a contact member for the participants so that they can access information regarding their health and the current course of the research. Paragraph (k) states that participants may withdraw their consent and leave the study at any time they wish. In addition, they may demand information regarding the data kept on himself/herself and also demand correction or deletion of such data. It is also emphasized that such demands shall not cause any loss of rights for the participant during his/her follow-up and treatment. Paragraph (m) addresses the issue of payments to the participants and states that apart from the insurance policy costs, any financial offer or any sort of such incentives aiming to persuade the volunteers is forbidden. The same article also affirms that the costs arising from the participation of volunteers in the study should be included in the study budget. Paragraph (ç) forbids any research that may disturb the genetic identity of the individual's germ cells. In paragraph (d), it is stated that the decisions regarding the treatments of volunteers in a research are to be determined by physicians and dentists. Last but not least, paragraph (n) emphasizes that the identity of the participants must be kept confidential during the publication of study results.

376. The importance and details of informed consent process for individuals offered to take part in drug research have also been addressed in Articles 32–36 of the RPR issued in 1998. Article 32 states that no one can be subject to medical interventions (which are of no therapeutic benefit and are aimed to serve the purposes of research, training or gaining experience) without their consent and the Ministry of Health's approval. Article 33 details the scope and content of disclosure in research, stating that the volunteer should be provided information with regard to the purpose, procedures, potential benefits and harms of the research. According to this article, a research may not be carried out if the potential harms associated with the research cannot be determined beforehand, and all precautions to ensure the protection of personal rights of participants have to be taken. The same article also states that the volunteer is to be informed that he/she can withdraw consent at any time at any stage of research. Article 34 states that informed consent in drug trials has to be obtained in written form and maximum care should be taken to ensure that the consent given by the participant is entirely based on his free will.

Furthermore, section 9 of the most recent GCP Guidelines (*see* paragraphs 374–376) has been entirely devoted to informed consent of the voluntary participant. All elements of informed consent, including disclosure of relevant information, voluntariness and written consent have been emphasized.

V. Drug Research on Minors, Pregnant Women, Incompetent Individuals and Other Vulnerable Populations

377. Article 6 of RCT addresses the issue of medical research on children and states that research on children is allowed on condition that:

- the subject of the research is directly related to children or a clinical entity that can only be examined if children are concerned;
- the results obtained in adults necessitate the study findings to be also proven in children;
- no serious risks for the participants are concerned; and
- the study is to provide direct benefits for the participants.

Paragraph (c) of Article 6 states that if the potential participant (the child) has decision-making capacity, then his/her decision about refusing or withdrawing consent at any stage of the study must be respected. It should be noted that RCT emphasizes the child's decision-making authority at this point and the previous regulation (RDT) was not so clear on this issue. In addition, paragraph (e) of the same article states that the relevant Ethics Committee, while reviewing research with children, will be notified about the clinical, ethical and psychosocial aspects of the study by a paediatrician and the study protocol will be evaluated accordingly.

378. Article 7 addresses the requirements for pregnant/breastfeeding women, and women who have recently given birth, whereas Article 8 addresses the status of legally restricted individuals. The requirements in this section are similar to those defined for research on children. Accordingly, research on these populations is possible only if the individuals will directly benefit from the study and unless there are no serious risks that can be foreseen.

Article 9 of RCT refers to a heterogeneous group of potentially vulnerable participants, which include incompetent individuals and patients in intensive care units. Accordingly, research on these individuals may be performed on condition that research is directly related to these individuals, or the clinical entity in question can only be observed in these populations, or, if no other available treatment option is present and a direct benefit to the individuals is to be expected. Nevertheless, the requirements listed below must also be fulfilled:

(a) The individual's and/or the legal representative's informed consent must be obtained.
(b) If the individual has decision-making capacity and refuses or withdraws consent, such decision must be respected.
(c) No serious risks for the individuals should be foreseen, or the benefits to the individual must outweigh the risks.
(d) Except for the coverage of inevitable costs arising from the participation of volunteers in the study, financial offers or any sort of such incentives aiming to persuade the volunteers are forbidden.

VI. Oviedo Convention on Human Research

379. The Oviedo Convention (Convention for the Protection of Human Rights and Dignity of the Human Being with Regard to the Application of Biology and Medicine: Convention on Human Rights and Biomedicine) states that under certain conditions, individuals who do not have the capacity to consent may be included in research. This issue has been addressed in Article 17 of the Convention, which is entitled 'Protection of persons not able to consent to research'.

VII. Medical Research in Criminal Law

380. Article 90 of the Turkish Penal Code states that medical research on humans can be conducted on condition that the individual consents to the procedure. Such consent must be obtained in written form and must be based on adequate disclosure of information regarding the content and the consequences of the process. The same article also indicates additional requirements along with the individual's consent. Accordingly, the permission of the relevant committees or authorities must have been obtained, the process must have been tested by in vitro studies and on an adequate number of animals and the scientific data obtained via these methods must show that research on humans is necessary in order to reach the desired purpose. In addition, the process should not leave any foreseeable harmful and permanent effect, it should not include any painful methods which may be incompatible with human dignity and the purpose intended to be reached by the process must outweigh any burdens and harms that might be imposed on the individual's health.

381. In its initial version, the third paragraph of Article 90 prohibited research on children. However, the paragraph was amended shortly thereafter, and the provision was replaced by newer provisions which allow such research within certain limits. Accordingly, children can be included in scientific research on condition that: (1) the scientific data obtained via other studies indicate that such research is necessary on children; (2) the consent of the children capable of expressing consent, in addition to his parents' or legal representative's written permission, is also obtained; and (3) the committees that will authorize such research to have a paediatrician among their members.

VIII. Developments Expected in the Near Future

382. A draft for a new regulation that is intended to replace the Regulation for Clinical Drug Trials has been on the Ministry of Health's agenda for several years now. In addition to proposing some changes for ethics committees (such as accreditation of ethics committees), the new regulation is also expected to have a broader scope, with special emphasis on important issues such as the protection of volunteers, minor and incompetent subjects and informed consent.

§6. The Use of Stem Cells for Therapeutic and Research Purposes

383. There is no specific legislation governing the use of stem cells in Turkey. However, an amendment to the RHCART was issued on 8 July 2005, stating that embryos produced during the assisted reproduction procedures may not be used for purposes other than assisted reproduction. Furthermore, embryonic stem cell research was banned in a circular issued by the Ministry of Health on 30 September 2005 *(30 Eylül 2005 tarihli ve 2005/141 sayılı Embriyonik Kök Hücre Araştırmalar Hakkında Sağlık Bakanlığı Genelgesi)*, and it has been stated in the circular that this prohibition would be in effect until the necessary ethical and scientific framework for the field has been established. For this purpose, the Ministry of Health established a scientific committee in 2006. This committee is now officially known as National Scientific Advisory Committee on Stem Cell Transfer *(Kök Hücre Nakilleri Bilimsel Danışma Kurulu)*. It is currently made up of twelve scholars (mostly from various fields of medicine, along with a professor in medical ethics and another one in public law).

384. The committee has prepared a number of guidelines entitled 'Non-embryonic stem cell research for therapeutic purposes'. The guidelines state the prerequisites for such research as in the following:

(a) Similar research must have been done in vitro or on animals of adequate number.
(b) The findings of such research must indicate that it is necessary to conduct such research on humans in order to achieve the intended purpose.
(c) The research must have no foreseeable harm and permanent effect on human health.

These guidelines have been issued by the Ministry of Health as appended to Circular No. 2006/51 dated 4 May 2006 of the Ministry of Health on Stem Cell Research *(4 Mayis 2006 tarihli ve 2006/51 sayılı Kök Hücre Çalışmaları Hakkında Sağlık Bakanlığı Genelgesi)*. They also emphasize the significance of an ethics committee review of the research and informed consent of the individuals prior to the initiation of the research. It is hoped that these guidelines will form the basis for the legislations to be issued to govern the activities in this new field in Turkey.

§7. Euthanasia

385. *See also* paragraph 145.

386. The Turkish Constitution states that every individual possesses fundamental rights and liberties that arise from the personal being of the individual (Article 12) and recognizes the inviolable and indefeasible status of such rights. Article 17 emphasizes the 'inviolability and physical and spiritual being' of individuals and states that everyone is entitled to the right to protect and improve his/her life and physical and spiritual being. Thus, the Constitution assigns an inviolable status to the life of the person and evaluates the concept from such a perspective.

387. In addition, the Turkish Penal Code and Turkish Civil Code also aim to protect personal rights and their inviolable status. Therefore, homicide is recognized as a criminal offence in the Penal Code, and the sanction to be imposed for such an act has been defined as heavy imprisonment. The Civil Code ensures the right to life, which is regarded as an essential part of personal rights. Article 23 of the Civil Code emphasizes the inviolable and indefeasible status of personal rights and thus ensures legal protection for the life of individuals.

388. Turkish legal doctrine defends the right to life as indefeasible and inalienable and even the individual himself/herself is not entitled to restrict its limits.[121] Therefore, terminating a patient's life to put an end to his/her suffering on his/her demand is forbidden in Turkish law. The individual's consent does not justify the unlawful status of such an act. In addition, it is observed that such interventions have been clearly prohibited in certain legislations. MDR's Article 13, paragraph 3, states that the physician is not allowed to perform interventions on a patient's demand when such interventions have no diagnostic or therapeutic purpose and will harm the physical and mental health of the patient. The Regulation on Patients' Rights also prohibits euthanasia and declares that individuals cannot waive the right to life due to medical or other reasons.

389. In a verdict by the High Court of Appeals, it has been clearly stated that euthanasia would be evaluated as intentional murder regardless of the patient's consent. Article 81 of the Turkish Penal Code (which does not include a specific provision for euthanasia) defines felony murder. Accordingly, ending an individual's life, even for the sake of ending his/her pain in the case of a fatal disease, will be addressed within the context defined in this article. In addition, Article 83 of the same Code defines negligent murder, where a person may cause another's death by inaction and states that such an act would also be evaluated as intentional murder. Items listed in the Code for such inaction (or act of omission) include situations where a person to whom certain duties have been imposed by way of legislative texts or contracts fails to act to carry out those duties. This provision applies to physicians since such obligations have been imposed on them in several legislations. For instance, Article 2 of MDR declares that the primary duty of the physician is to provide due care with regard to health, life and personality. Therefore, it is understood that the physician is obligated to take the necessary precautions for the protection of the patient's life since he/she has a legal obligation to protect the individual's life. Furthermore, RPR also includes a provision (Article 14) on the physician's duty to save the life of the patient and to take the necessary precautions for this purpose. If the individual dies as a consequence of the physician's inaction where he/she does not perform a medical intervention, then it could be argued that

121. Inceoğlu, *supra* para. 104, n. 3, s. 79.

the physician will have violated the provisions in the aforementioned texts. Within this scheme, the physician could be charged based on the provisions provided in Article 83 of the Penal Code.

390. Another controversial provision in Turkish law with regard to euthanasia exists in the RPR. According to this legislation, patients have the right to refuse and stop treatment. However, the Regulation states that after the initiation of a treatment, the patient can only refuse a treatment when the refusal has no medical drawbacks. This statement can be considered to limit the right to refuse treatment under certain conditions. Therefore, under life-threatening medical conditions, the physician has an obligation to intervene even if the patient refuses, and this framework can also be considered to prohibit passive euthanasia.

§8. Transsexual Interventions

391. Turkish law allows transsexual operations on condition that certain requirements have been fulfilled. There are basically two requirements for such a procedure: The first one has to be fulfilled prior to surgery and the other one should be fulfilled following it. Turkish Civil Code's Article 40 addresses the process as in the following:

> The person demanding a sex change can do so by applying a court of peace and ask for approval. However, such approval can only be granted on condition that the person has fully attained 18 years of age, is not married, and possesses a report prepared by a formal health committee of a public hospital which states that the person is of transsexual nature, permanently lacks the ability to reproduce, and that such sex change is a medical necessity for the mental health of the individual.

Following the sex change surgery, the person may apply to the court for the formal approval of appropriate correction in the population registry. Civil Code Article 40 addresses the procedure as in the following:

> When the proper sex change surgery, performed in accordance with the granted approval and in parallel with medically appropriate methods, is verified by a formal health committee report of a public hospital, the court shall decide to make the appropriate corrections in the population registry.

§9. Prenatal Diagnosis and Other Genetic-Related Issues

I. Prenatal Diagnosis

392. Based on the Health Care Services Law (*Umumi Hıfzısıhha Kanunu*), the Regulation on Diagnostic Centres for Genetic Diseases (*Genetik Hastalıklar Tanı Merkezleri Yönetmeliği*) was issued in 1998. While this Regulation mostly focuses on the technical and professional competency of the centres, the consent of the individual in the process of obtaining relevant samples and the confidentiality of the genetic information is also emphasized. In addition, a sample consent form has been added at the end of the text as a guide for healthcare professionals. This regulation was repealed with the regulation of the same name published on 10 January 2020.

II. Genetic Research and the Human Genome

393. While there is no specific regulation on genetic research in Turkey, it should be noted that Oviedo Convention became a part of Turkey's national legislation in 2003. The Convention includes articles on the human genome, and they have been adopted without any exceptions.

A. Turkey Scientific and Technological Research Institution's DNA Bank

394. Turkey Scientific and Technological Research Institution (TUBITAK) DNA/Cell Bank was established in 1994 through a scientific grant from TTGV (Technology Development Fund of Turkey). The main aim of the Bank is to create a registry of biological samples from families affected with rare genetic disorders. In addition, the Bank also aims to address the ethical, legal and social implications of biobanking.[122]

§10. Traditional and Complementary Medicine

395. Early examples of regulation about traditional and complementary medicine practices go back to *Resmi Gazete* 29 May 1991 Acupuncture Treatment Regulation (*Akupunktur Tedavi Yönetmeliği*) (ATR). This regulation was reissued on 17 September 2002.[123] On 21 August 2010, *Sağlık Bakanlığı Sertifikalı Eğitim Yönetmeliği* (Ministry of Health Certified Education Regulation) gave the mainframe of standards of Phytotherapy practice by physicians. With an additional article (Article 9) to LPOMRA on 6 April 2011, it can only be practised by physicians and dentists (only in dental care) who have a 'practice certificate' in specific area, in a unit or practice centres authorized by Ministry of Health. Other healthcare professions can help certified physicians at the centres and units.

Practices can be realized in 'practice units' in state and private healthcare centres and 'practice centres' in university and education and research hospitals.

---

122. Akay G. G., Karabulut H., G. Tükün A, Bilim ve Teknik Ocak 2012. Biyobankalar Nedir Neye Hizmet Ederler https://services.tubitak.gov.tr/edergi/yazi.pdf;jsessionid=5C8Spwf+rWEtfenikeehGaO+?dergiKodu=4&cilt=45&sayi=758&sayfa=48&yaziid=32687.
123. Sert, G. & M. Karataş, 'Alternatif Tıp Uygulamalarında Türk Hukukunun Yaklaşımı' (*Approach of Turkish Law to Alternative Medicine Practices*) *Açık Sayfa Aylık Aktüel Hukuk Dergisi* May 2004: 55: 27–30.

Ministry of Health is authorized to control every traditional and complementary medicine practice as per 2 November 2011 regulation. Depending on that authorization, Ministry of Health enacted Traditional and Complementary Medicine Practices Regulation on 27 October 2014.[124]

§11. Remote Health Services (Telemedicine)

396. Telemedicine which provides healthcare services through contemporary medical technology regardless of location and geography, was regulated in the RPRHS dated 10 February 2022. The scope of the telemedicine service, the procedures and principles regarding the license process and inspection of the healthcare facilities were regulated in the relevant regulation. The provisions of the regulation are carried out by the MoH. The MoH is also authorized to eliminate the hesitations and disruptions that may arise from the implementation of the regulation.

397. The regulation covers healthcare facilities providing remote healthcare services, healthcare professionals, remote healthcare information system developers, and real persons who wish to receive healthcare services remotely. In cases where there is no provision in the regulation, the legislation on patient rights and the protection of personal data will be applied.

Healthcare services that can be provided as telemedicine services are specified in Article 7 of the regulation. According to the regulation, the person requesting remote health service can be examined to the extent that the remote health service allows, and the person can be evaluated by medical observation and follow-up. In addition, it is possible to control the diseases diagnosed with remote health service, to give medical advice, consultation or secondary opinion. The regulation also allows performing interventional or surgical operations determined by the MoH, provided that the technological possibilities allow and the necessary permissions are obtained from the MoH.

398. The regulation also allows the necessary medical procedures to protect the health of individuals in line with national guidelines in endemic or epidemic outbreaks. In addition, the regulation allows the measurement and tracking of wearable technologies and other medical devices and the health data of the person requesting health services as well. Moreover, the regulation also includes the preparation of e-prescription and e-report for the patient evaluated by the physician.

399. RPRHS, besides the above-mentioned topics, also includes provisions on international health tourism. Accordingly, health facilities that have received an international health tourism authorization certificate will be able to provide remote health services within the scope of international health tourism and tourists health

---

124. O.N. Karahancı et al., Geleneksel ve Tamamlayıcı Tıp Uygulamaları Yönetmeliği ile Yönetmelik Taslağı'nın Karşılaştırılması (*Comparison of Traditional, Complementary Medicine Draft Regulations and Regulations*) *Turkish Journal of Bioethics*. 2015; 2(2): 117–126 | DOI: 10.5505/tjob.2015.85856.

within the framework of the relevant legislation. In addition, the Regulation allows the healthcare facility to provide remote healthcare services to a healthcare provider in another healthcare facility, provided that it has an authorized license in the same branch.

I. Informing the Patient

400. The issue of informing the person who will receive remote health services is included in the Article 9 of the Regulation. Accordingly, the person who will receive remote healthcare services should be informed before the remote healthcare service is started. The person will be informed in a plain language that can be understood to the extent that it is suitable for the nature of the health service to be provided:

In the regulation, the topics that the patient will be informed about are listed as follows:

- Identity and expertise, if any, of the healthcare professional who will provide remote healthcare services.
- The healthcare professional will not be physically in the same environment.
- Remote health service cannot be the equivalent of face-to-face health care.
- Distance health services and applied treatments are different.
- It is not possible to benefit from remote health services, if that will disrupt an ongoing treatment.
- The patient should be informed that, in emergency cases, it is necessary to apply to the nearest emergency service instead of the remote health service.
- Fee of the remote health service, the scope of the service to be provided, whether the service will be covered under any health insurance.
- It is forbidden to record audio or video regarding remote health service delivery without the express consent of the parties; however, the records regarding the health services received in accordance with the legislation on the processing of personal health data will be kept and transferred to the MoH information system in accordance with the personal data protection legislation and privacy.
- Patient should be informed that, he/she should be allowed to access his/her camera and/or microphone in order to start the remote health service delivery.
- In case the audio and/or video cannot be transmitted between the parties, the remote health service may not start, and if it has started, it may not be continued.
- Remote health service can be terminated at any time by informing the other party for medical or legal reasons.
- The person providing remote health care is personally responsible for ensuring the security of the information systems, user names and passwords used in the delivery of remote health care services.
- The patient should be informed about the nature and results of the health service to be provided by remote health care services.

401. In the relevant article, it is also stated that the general procedures and principles regarding the obligation to fulfil within the scope of health service provision are reserved. In this context, without prejudice to the issues stipulated by the disclosure obligation, it is seen that the issues that may arise from the nature of the remote health service itself and that may require information are stipulated in the relevant article.[125]

II. Protection of Personal Data and Registration

402. In the RPRHS, it is stated that the healthcare facility and healthcare professionals are responsible for the protection of patients' privacy and personal data in the provision of healthcare services. It is emphasized that the personal data obtained through the services offered in the regulation will be processed in accordance with the legislation and all kinds of technical and administrative measures will be taken to ensure the security of this data.

According to the regulation, only with the explicit consent of the parties, video or audio recordings of the remote health services provided within the scope of this regulation can be provided. It is also stated in the regulation that these records can be kept for a maximum of twelve months in the health facility providing remote health services or in secure data centres permitted by the MoH. The data should be deleted at the end of this period. In addition, according to the regulation, authorities authorized by law and Ministry inspectors within the scope of an administrative investigation will have access to these records.

403. According to the regulation, transactions related to remote health services will be recorded in digital environment and the recorded data will be sent to the central health data system of the MoH within the framework of the procedures and principles determined by the MoH in accordance with the relevant legislation, without prejudice to the exceptional regulations in the legislation on the protection of personal data.

III. Rights and Liabilities of the Parties

404. According to the regulation, the person receiving remote health services must explain the requested information about his medical history and health status to the healthcare professional in an accurate and understandable way.

405. In addition, the person who receives remote healthcare services or healthcare professional should inform the other party about the existence of the third person if there is a third person who can see and/or hear the interview. The organization providing remote health services is obliged to ensure that, the healthcare professional providing healthcare services has sufficient knowledge and equipment to provide remote healthcare services.

---

125. Z. Akgün, Evaluation of the Regulation on Providing Remote Healthcare Services, *Turkish Journal of Bioethics.* 8 (4):194–198 (2022) pp 196.

Part III. The Physician in Relation to the Healthcare System

Chapter 1. Collegial Relationships

§1. Associations

406. Physicians, pharmacists and dentists have professional associations in Turkey. Each of the associations has its own law (TPAL, Turkish Dental Association Law (TDAL) and Turkish Pharmacists Association Law), governing the association's structure and function. These laws also contain provisions regarding the professional disciplinary liability. HDBs, which are included among the fundamental organs of such associations, review and resolve complaints arising from conflicts between member colleagues and between colleagues and other individuals.

§2. Healthcare Centres

I. Healthcare Service Institutions

407. Healthcare institutions in Turkey exist in both the public and the private sectors. Legislation governing public healthcare service has already been discussed (*see* paragraphs 21–28). The institutions detailed below, and legislations governing these institutions, mostly apply to the private sector; however, some of those institutions may also be operated in the public sector and relevant provisions apply in such cases, as outlined below.

A. *Institutions Providing Diagnostic and Therapeutic Healthcare Service*

1. Institutions Providing Private Outpatient Healthcare

408. The new 'Regulation on Private Diagnostic and Therapeutic Outpatient Health Care Institutions' (*Ayakta Teşhis ve Tedavi Yapılan Özel Sağlık Kuruluşları Hakkında Yönetmelik)* (RPDTOHC) issued in 2008 supersedes the previous regulation of the same name dating from 2000.

409. The new RPDTOHC enacted in 2008 was amended in 2009 and 2010. The number of types of healthcare establishments defined in the previous Regulation has been narrowed down to three basic structures: medical centres, private outpatient clinics and private physician offices.

a. Medical Centres

410. Medical centres must employ at least four specialists from the branches of clinical medicine, and their service should be adjusted in line with the requirements set forth in the Regulation. Medical centres may be established by a physician qualified for private practice or through the partnership of multiple physicians or dentists. Applications to the Ministry of Health can be filed in line with the planning requirements of the Ministry.

411. Dentistry services may also be provided in these centres. However, the Regulation requires the presence of a separate unit for each dentist employed.

412. The new Regulation has defined a number of specifications regarding the locations and properties of the buildings where the establishments in question will be opened. For instance, buildings of medical centres may not be used for other purposes; they have to be self-contained structures specific to the centre.

b. Outpatient Clinics

413. According to the Regulation, an outpatient clinic is an establishment that can be founded by at least two physicians and their service units must be directly connected. They can be opened by physicians qualified to provide outpatient healthcare service on condition that they work as partners and provide service within the outpatient clinic.

c. Private Offices

414. Private offices, however, are run by a physician only to provide the services unique to his/her profession. Surgical and invasive procedures cannot be performed in these offices.

415. It should also be noted that any type of advertising activities by any of the institutions that are subject to the Regulation has been prohibited by the RPDTOHC.

2. Outpatient Diagnostic and Therapeutic Healthcare in Public Institutions

416. Turkish law includes provisions allowing outpatient healthcare for diagnostic and therapeutic purposes to be provided in certain institutions and establishments, including municipalities and the Turkish Red Crescent (*Kızılay*). These services are also subject to the regulations mentioned above. In addition, private law provisions also apply to the contracts made in these institutions.

3. Institutions Providing Inpatient Treatment Services

a. Private Hospitals

417. Private hospitals are not a part of public administration. Their purpose is to provide healthcare service for treatment and rehabilitation, as well as birth care services, as defined in Private Hospitals Law (*Hususi Hastaneler Kanunu*) (PHL) issued in the RG on 5 June 1933, No. 2419.

Opening a private hospital is subject to the Ministry of Health's approval. The administrator of the private hospital can be a natural person or a legal person as a society, foundation or a trading corporation.

Administration of the hospital is carried out by the hospital administrator. The management duty can also be performed by the administrator; in such a case, the administrator must be a physician with a minimum of five-year working experience and two years of this service must have been served at a hospital. The exceptions to this are the managers of mental care hospitals, and hospitals providing specialized healthcare in the field of paediatrics and obstetrics. Managers of such institutions must be specialists trained in the relevant field of medicine. In addition, the manager in charge of tuberculosis hospitals must be an internal medicine specialist. Hospital managers are responsible for ensuring that healthcare service provided to patients is compatible with the current standards of medical sciences.

Rules regarding the establishment and operation of private hospitals have been defined in the Primary Regulation on Private Hospitals (*Özel Hastaneler Tüzüğü*) (issued in Official Journal No. 17924, dated 10 January 1983) and in RPH (*Özel Hastaneler Yönetmeliği*) (issued in Official Journal No. 24708, dated 27 March 2002).

Chapter 2. Relationships with Other Healthcare Providers

§1. Pharmacists

I. Background

418. In addition to pharmacies, there were several other providers where drugs could be purchased during the Ottoman Empire era. Following the death of some individuals due to drugs obtained from such alternative providers, the need for a regulation *(mismanage)* was recognized and it was issued in 1852. The legitimate control mechanism over the practice of pharmacy was thus initiated, and this process has been continued by adapting legislations in accordance with the requirements of the day.[126]

II. Requirements for Opening a Pharmacy

A. *Law on Pharmacies and Pharmacists*

1. Diploma

419. The law enacted in 1953, entitled 'Law on Pharmacies and Pharmacists' (*Eczacılar ve Eczaneler Hakkında Kanun*) (LOPP), necessitates the possession of a diploma obtained from the Turkish School of Pharmacy or from other faculties of pharmacy. In addition, such a diploma has to be approved by the Ministry of Health, as stated in Article 2.

2. Citizenship

420. Article 2 of LOPP states that the individual demanding to open a pharmacy has to be a Turkish citizen.

---

126. For a detailed review of the history of legislations regarding pharmacy and development of state control over the education and practice of pharmacy, *see* N. Yıldırım & G. Sert, 'Eczacılık Mevzuatımızın Tarihsel Sürecinde Eczane Açma/Eczacı Olma Koşulları ve Hekim-Eczacı İlişkisi' *(Requirements for Opening Pharmacies and Practicing as a Pharmacist and the Pharmacist-Physician Relationship Within the History of Our Pharmacy Legislations),* VII. Türk Eczacılık Tarihi Toplantısı. 27–28 Mayıs 2005 Ankara Bildiri Kitabı *(to be published);* N. Yıldırım, 'Dârülfünûn-ı Osmanî Tıp Fakültesi Eczacı Mektebi Öğrencilerine Ait Kabulnâmeler ve Şehâdetnâmeler' *(Diplomas and Documents of the Students of the School of Pharmacy of Ottoman Medicine Faculty).* II. *Türk Tıp Tarihi Kongresi, Kongreye Sunulan Bildiriler. Türk Tarih Kurumu Basımevi* (Ankara 1999), s. 245 (239–279 ve 65–100); N. Yıldırım, 'Nizamnâme-i Eczacıyan Der Memalik-i Osmaniye, Osmanlı Devleti'nde Eczacılar Nizamnâmesi-1852' *(Regulation on Pharmacists in the Ottoman Empire).* IV. Türk Eczacılık Tarihi Toplantısı Bildirileri (İstanbul, 4–5 Haziran 1998). Ed. E. Dölen (İstanbul 2000) ss 43–44.

3. Criminal Record Requirements

421. According to LOPP, the individual demanding to open a pharmacy should not have been convicted of certain criminal offences. Such offences include criminal sentences for infamous crimes, heavy imprisonment for three years or more, any freedom-restricting conviction applied for professional wrongdoing of one year or longer duration, temporary ban from the practice of pharmacy for two times in a five-year period (due to offences conducted by abusing the privileges of the profession). Individuals with any of these offences in their criminal record are not entitled to open a pharmacy, as stated in Article 4 of LOPP.

4. Restriction of Access for Certain Groups

422. Article 17 of LOPP states that members of the Armed Forces and state clerks may not open a pharmacy.

B. The Physician–Pharmacist Relationship

423. The legislations prior to LOPP (before 1953) focused on appropriate preparation of drugs compatible with the physician's prescription and this formed the main framework of the physician–pharmacist relationship. According to these legislations, prescriptions with no physician signature were considered invalid and such drugs were not to be provided. In addition, issues such as corrections marked in the prescription, and the procedures to follow in case of a drug prescribed at an overdose level and for contacting the physician were addressed in these documents.

424. LOPP issued in 1953 allows physicians in the public sector and in freelance practice and veterinaries to possess a pharmacy cabinet in case a pharmacy does not exist in the area, as stated in Article 14. In addition, LOPP forbids corrections in prescriptions in Article 25. Accordingly, pharmacists have to first contact the physician before preparing prescriptions that include overdose levels of a drug, and prescriptions that have not been signed by the physician. However, if the treating physician cannot be contacted, then the pharmacist should prepare the drug at the maximum level allowed in the codex and should inform the highest-ranking health authority of the local area.

425. Furthermore, Article 37 of LOPP states that physicians may not admit patients in a pharmacy; however, emergency medical care may be provided in case of an accident or unexpected danger.

C. Turkish Pharmacists Deontology Regulation

426. Turkish Pharmacists Deontology Regulation (*Türk Eczacıları Deontoloji Tüzüğü*) was issued on 27 July 1986. This regulation addresses the principles and rules to be followed by pharmacists with regard to deontology. Articles 1–2 state that the primary duty of the pharmacists is to work in absolute cooperation with colleagues, physicians and veterinaries and respect and care for human and animal health.

Article 3 states that pharmacists are obligated to show the maximum amount of care during the preparation of the drugs in the prescriptions and while handing the drugs to the prescription owner. In addition, Article 4 of the Regulation states that the pharmacists may not disclose the confidential information obtained during the practice of pharmacy, unless required to do so by the law.

Furthermore, Article 5 affirms that the pharmacist may not provide drugs other than those written in the prescription, and may not give recommendations to the patient or to the patient's relatives apart from the directives of the physician.

The Regulation also bans advertisement activities for pharmacists. They may not use middlemen in their activities or utilize promotion activities during the sale of drugs. Last but not least, Article 8 of the Regulation states that pharmacists may not prevent patients from exercising their right to choose their own pharmacy.

§2. Dentists

I. Introduction

427. The practise of dentistry in Turkey is regulated within the framework of medicine. Legislations such as the LPOMRA and MDR (*Tıbbi Deontoloji Tüzüğü*) include common provisions that apply for both practices of medicine and dentistry. The practice of dentistry has been limited to oral and dental care in LPOMRA. The requirements for practising dentistry in Turkey are the same as those for practising medicine. In addition, Turkish Dental Association (TDA) was founded with the TDAL issued on 25 June 1985, which requires dentists to register to be able to practise dentistry.

II. Turkish Dental Association Law

428. According to TDAL, a Chamber of Dentists has to be established in any province having at least 100 dentists registered to the association in their area of jurisdiction. The organs of the chambers have been defined in Articles 4 and 5 as the Chamber General Board, Chamber Executive Board, Chamber DB and Chamber Inspection Board. The General Board is the highest decision-making authority of the Chamber and consists of the dentists registered in the board.

429. Chamber Executive Board is chosen for a two-year period among the members of the General Board. Articles 9–11 of TDAL define the duties of the board as in the following: to apply the decisions of the association and Chamber General Board; to help in implementing the professional codes and provisions of the relevant legislations; to prevent commissioning and advertisement activities in the practice of dentistry; to take the necessary precautions to ensure ongoing professional training for colleagues; to take part as a negotiator or referee for the resolution of conflicts encountered during dentist–dentist and dentist–patient relationships.

430. The DB of the Chamber is elected among the members of the relevant chamber for a two-year period. In order to be eligible for DB membership, the member should have at least ten years of dental practice experience (in addition to the general criteria for election as defined in TDAL). The duty of the DB is to review the cases that require disciplinary prosecution (as decided by the Chamber's General Board), to decide on the appropriate disciplinary sanction that should be imposed and to use its authority for other responsibilities as defined by TDAL (Articles 13 and 14).

431. TDA consists of all Chambers of Dentists established throughout Turkey, as stated in Article 19 of TDAL.

432. TDA General Board consists of the delegates elected by the general boards of all chambers and full members of the central organs of TDA (who are natural members of the TDA General Board) and the presidents of the chambers, as stated in Article 21. HDB of TDA is elected by the General Board among its delegates for a period of two years; it has nine full-time and nine substitute members (Article 28 of TDAL). Article 29 of TDAL states that HDB of TDA's duty is to review the objections made against the decisions of DBs of the chambers and to use its authority for other responsibilities defined by TDAL.

§3. Nurses and Midwives

I. Nurses

433. In order to qualify to practise the nursing profession in Turkey, the individual must be a Turkish citizen and must receive the required training by graduating from the relevant schools, as stated in Nursing Law (*Hemşirelik Kanunu*) issued in 1954. The law was amended very recently in 2007 (Law No. 5634, RG: 02.05.2007). Several articles were removed and the standards for practising nursing were redefined. Accordingly, individuals must have a diploma from a faculty of nursing or a higher school of nursing of a university and their diploma has to be approved by the Ministry of Health. The mentioned schools and faculties should offer four years of nursing education and training. In addition, individuals trained in a foreign country (in a school of nursing recognized by the Ministry) may also practice as a nurse, on condition that the equivalent status of their training and diploma is approved by the Ministry.

434. According to Article 4 of Nursing Law, nurses have an obligation to apply the treatments stated in writing by physicians except in emergency situations. In addition, they are defined as the healthcare personnel responsible for planning, providing, inspecting and evaluating nursing care.

435. Article 5 of Nursing Law states that nurses may freely practice their profession. Nurses willing to engage in private practice have the duty to notify the highest-ranking health officer of the state.

436. The RAIHI (*Yataklı Tedavi Kurumları İşletme Yönetmeliği*) includes provisions about the duties and responsibilities of nurses. According to this Regulation, nurses are to take part in patient care and treatment procedures in accordance with the framework defined by the physicians.

II. Midwives

437. Articles 47–57 of LPOMRA primarily have provisions addressing midwives. Accordingly, being a Turkish citizen is a prerequisite for practising this profession in Turkey. Possessing a diploma from one of the schools of midwifery (either from those within a faculty of medicine or those within the framework of Ministry of Health) and having this diploma approved by the Ministry of Health are the other legally determined requirements. RAIHI defines a midwife as the person who is a graduate of a school of healthcare and is equipped with the necessary skills to carry out the tasks regarding birth and birth control.

438. LPOMRA states that individuals wishing to practise midwifery should notify the highest-ranking health officer of the area. This same law authorizes midwives to examine and provide healthcare for pregnant women during pregnancy and normal labour. However, midwives are not allowed to intervene in other labour situations where interventions with medical instruments are indicated. In such cases, the midwives are obligated to call a physician. RAIHI defines the duties of midwives in more detail. Accordingly, midwives assigned to provide care during labour in healthcare institutions, within the limits of their professional authority, are expected to take the necessary precautions and perform preparatory processes needed to ensure a healthy delivery. They examine the mother and the child, and particularly take note of the heart sounds of the baby, perform a genital examination of the mother if necessary and thus monitor the pregnant women during the course of pregnancy. The same regulation also notes in its Article 133 that midwives assist the pregnant women during normal delivery, but they have to notify a specialist physician immediately in cases of problematic pregnancies or in cases where they are unable to identify the exact medical condition. Similarly, midwives have to note the medical information (such as gender, length, head circumference, thorax circumference, physical abnormalities, signs of hereditary disease, the properties of placenta and umbilical cord) about the newborns following the delivery of the baby. In cases of multiple pregnancies, such as twins, they take note of the time interval between the delivery of the babies, and in stillborn babies, they check and take note of whether there is spontaneous breathing.

439. In addition to these tasks, midwives can also provide other services delivered by the nurses and are subject to provisions that apply to nurses in the context of healthcare institutions. Midwives with special training in family planning also have a duty to provide information and counselling to families about birth control.

440. It has been stated in LPOMRA that midwives are allowed to possess drugs which they may require during their practice. However, midwives are not allowed to prescribe drugs. LPOMRA states that midwives can procure the drugs on a prescription filled out by any physician in the public sector.

Selected Bibliography

Akıncı, Ş. Türk Özel Hukukunda İnsan Kökenli Biyolojik Madde (Organ-Doku) Nakli Kavramı Ve Bundan Doğan Hukuki Sonuçlar *(The Concept of Biological Materials of Human Origin in Turkish Private Law and Legal Consequences).* Ankara: Yetkin Yay, 1996.

Aşçıoğlu, Ç. Tıbbi Yardım ve El Atmalardan Doğan Sorumluluklar *(Liabilities Arising from Medical Care and Medical Interventions).* Ankara, 1993.

Atabek, E.M. Tıbbi Deontoloji Konuları *(Medical Deontology Topics).* İstanbul: 1983.

Atabek, R. Hastanelerin Sorumluluğu *(Liability of Hospitals).* İstanbul Barosu Dergisi ss 628–650: 10: 11: 12: 60: 1986.

Atabek, R. & M. Sezen. Hekimin Mes'uliyeti *(Physician Liability).* İstanbul: Barosu Dergisi. 39: ss 135–166: 1954.

Ayan, M. Tıbbi Müdahalelerden Doğan Hukuki Sorumluluk *(Civil Liability Arising from the Medical Intervention).* Ankara: Kazancı Matbaası, 1991.

Bayraktar, K. Hekimin Tedavi Nedeni ile Cezai Sorumluluğu *(Criminal Liability of the Physician for Treatment).* İstanbul: İ.Ü. Yayınları, Sermet Matbaası, 1972.

Belgesay, M.R. Tıbbi Mesuliyet *(Medical Liability).* İstanbul: İ.Ü. Yayınları, 1954.

Çokar, M. Dünyada ve Türkiye'de İsteyerek Düşüğün Yasal Boyutunun Etik Açıdan Değerlendirilmesi *(Ethical Evaluation of the Legal Aspect of Voluntary Abortion in Turkey and in the World).* Doktora Tezi *(PhD thesis, soon to be published),* İstanbul: Marmara Üniversitesi Sağlık Bilimleri Enstitüsü, Doktora Tezi, 2006; Danışman: *(Mentor)* Şefik Görkey.

Değer, M. & E.M. Atabek. Tıbbi Deontoloji Konuları *(Medical Deontology Topics).* I˙stanbul: İ.Ü. Yay, 2000.

Donay, S. Meslek Sırrının Açiklanması Suçu *(The Offence of Disclosing Professional Secret).* İstanbul: İ.Ü. Yayınları Sulhi Goran Matbaası Varisleri Koll Şti., 1978.

Epöztürk, K. et al., 1998 Tarihli Hasta Hakları Yönetmeliği'nde 2014 Yılında Yapılan Değişikliklerin Tıp Etiği ve Hukuku Açısından İncelenmesi (*Evaluation of the Amendment of Patient's Rights Regulation of 1998 in 2014 from Ethical and Legal Perspectives*) (Oral Presentation) Vth National Veterinary History and Ethics Symposium 25–27 May 2016 Bursa. Abstracts. Eds T Özkul – S Erer., p. 54.

Erman, B. Tıbbi Müdahalenin Hukuka Uygunluğu *(Lawfulness of the Medical Intervention).* Ankara: Seçkin Yayınları, 2003.

Görkey, Ş. Gebeliğin Sonlandırılmasında Karşılaşılan Etik Sorunlar *(Ethical Issues Encountered During the Termination of Pregnancy).* Ed.: H. Hatemi, Doğan Yüce H., Medikal Etik (Doğum, Ölüm Süreçleri ve Yaşamın Anlamı). İstanbul: Reklam Yayım Dağıtım A.Ş., 2001, ss 80–109.

Helvacı, S. Türk ve İsviçre Hukuklarında Kişilik Haklarını Koruyucu Davalar *(Lawsuits on the Protection of Personal Rights in Turkish and Swiss Law).* İstanbul: Beta Basım A.Ş., 2001.

İnceoğlu, S. Ötanazi. Ölme hakkı (*Euthanasia. The Right to Die).* İstanbul: Ayrıntı Yayinları, 1999.

İpekyüz, F.Y. Türk Hukukunda Hekimlik Sözleşmesi *(Physician Contract in Turkish Law).* İstanbul: Vedat Kitapçılık, 2006.

Karahancı, O.N. et al., Geleneksel ve Tamamlayıcı Tıp Uygulamaları Yönetmeliği ile Yönetmelik Taslağı'nın Karşılaştırılması (*Comparison of Traditional, Complementary Medicine Draft Regulations and Regulations*) TJOB Turkish Journal of Bioethics. 2015; 2(2): 117–126 I DOI: 10.5505/tjob.2015.85856.

Karasu, S. Hekimin Sır Saklama Yükümlülüğü *(Physicians Duty to Maintain Confidentiality).* M.Ü. Sosyal Bilimler Enstitüsü Hukuk Anabilim Dalı Özel Hukuk Bilim Dalı Yüksek Lisans Tezi *(Unpublished M.Sc. Thesis),* İstanbul: 2005. Danışman (*Mentor*) Doç. Dr Serap Helvacı.

Kıyak, Y. Lectures on Medical Ethics Marmara Üniversitesi Yayın No. 445, İstanbul: Tıp Fakültesi Yayın No. 1, 1987.

Kunter, N., F. Yenisey & A. Nuhoğlu. Muhakeme Dalı Olarak Ceza Muhakemesi Hukuku *(Criminal Trial Law).* 15. İstanbul: Bası, Beta A.Ş., 2006.

Özdemir, H. Özel Hukukta Teşhis ve Tedavi Sözleşmesi (*Treatment Contract in Private Law*). Ankara: Yetkin Yayınları, 2004.

Özsunay, E. Alman ve Türk Hukuklarında Hekimin Hastayı Aydınlatma Ödevi ve İstisnaları *(The Duty of the Physician to Inform the Patient and the Exceptions to This Duty in German and Turkish Law).* MHAUM, Sorumluluk Hukukundaki Yeni Gelişmeler V. Sempozyumu, Türk Hukukunda Hekimin Hukuki ve Cezai Sorumluluğu, Ankara: 12/13 March 1982; Istanbul: Fakülteler Matbaası, 1983.

Öztürkler, C. Hukuk Uygulamasında Tıbbi Sorumluluk, Teşhis, Tedavi ve Tıbbi Müdahaleden Doğan Tazminat Davaları *(Lawsuits Arising from Medical Liability, Diagnosis and Medical Intervention in Legal Practice)* 1. Basım, Seçkin Yayıncılık A.Ş., Ankara: Kasım, 2003.

Reisoğlu, S. Hekimlerin Hukuki Sorumluluğu. Sorumluluk Hukukundaki Yeni Gelişmeler *(Civil Liability of Physicians. New developments in Liability Law).* İstanbul: V. Sempozyumu, 1983.

Sarıal, M.E. Sağlararası Organ Nakillerinden Doğan Hukuksal İlişkiler (*Legal Relations Arising from Organ Transplantations Between Living Persons*). İstanbul, 1986.

Savaş, H. Sağlık Çalışanlarının ve Sağlık Kurumlarının Tıbbi Müdahaleden Doğan Sorumluluklari *(The Liabilities of Health Care Workers and Health Care Institutions in Medical Interventions).* 1, Ankara: Baskı, Seçkin Yayıncılık, 2007.

Sert, G. Hasta Hakları – Uluslararası Bildirgeler ve Tıp Etiği Açısından – *(Patient Rights from the Perspective of International Documents and Medical Ethics),* İstanbul: Babil Yayınları, 2004.

Sert, G. Sağlık Hizmetlerinde Meslek Sirri ve Tanıklıktan Çekinme *(Confidentiality and Refusal of Testimony in Health Care).* Türkiye Biyoetik Derneği Uluslararası Katılımlı 3. Ulusal Tıp Etiği Kongresi Kongre Kitabı. Ed: Erdemir, A.D., Uzel, İ., Öncel, Ö., Oğuz, Y., Aksoy, Ş., Şahinoğlu, S., Kadıoğlu, S., Büken, N.Ö., Doğan, H., Yetener, M., Atıcı, E.C. 2. Bursa, 2003, ss 851–862.

Sert, G., T. Guvn & S. Gorkey. 'When Organ Donation from Living Donors Serves as the Main Source of Organ Procurement: A Critical Examination of the Ethical and Legal Challenges to Turkey's Recent Efforts to Overcome Organ Shortage.' *Transplantation Proceedings* 45 (2013): 2102–2105.

Sert, G. & M. Karataş. 'Alternatif Tıp Uygulamalarında Türk Hukukunun Yaklaşımı' (*Approach of Turkish Law to Alternative Medicine Practices*) *Açık Sayfa Aylık Aktüel Hukuk Dergisi* May 2004: 55: 27–30.

Tandoğan, H. Borçlar Hukuku Özel Borş İlişkileri *(Obligations Law Private Obligation Relations).* Ankara: Olgaç Matbaası, 1982.

Taşkın, A. Organ ve Doku Nakillerinde Hekimin Cezai Sorumluluğu *(Criminal Liability of the Physician in Organ and Tissue Transplantation).* Ankara: Adil Yayınevi, 1997.

Tekinay, S., et al., Tekinay, Borçlar Hukuku Genel Hükümler *(Obligations Law General Provisions),* 7, İstanbul: Baskı, Filiz Kitabevi, 1993.

Teziç, E. Anayasa Hukuku *(Constitutional Law).* 5. Istanbul: bası, Beta Basımevi, 1998.

The Constitution of Republic of Turkey in English. Office of the Prime Minister. Directorate of General Press and Information: Available at: www.byegm.gov.tr/mevzuat/anayasa/anayasa-ing.htm.

Türk Tabipler Birliği Hekimlik Meslek Etiği Kuralları (*Professional Code of Ethics of Turkish Physicians Association),* Ankara: Türk Tabipler Birliği Merkez Konseyi, Yorum Matbaacılık, 2002.

Tüzmen, Ş. Avukatlıkta Meslek Sırrını İfşa Suçu *(The Offence of Disclosing Professional Secret for Lawyers),* Ankara: Barosu Dergisi, 1–2: 115–128: 1962.

Ünver, Y. Avrupa Biyo-Hukuk Sözleşmesinin Türk Hukukuna Etkileri *(The Effects of European Bioethics Convention on Turkish Law).* Kamu Hukuku Arşivi, Akademik Araştırma ve Dayanışma Derneği Yayını Ed. M. Avcı, 8: 2, ss 182–198. Kasım, 2005.

Ünver, Y. Ceza Hukukunda İzin Verilen Risk *(Allowed Risk in Criminal Law),* 1, İstanbul: Baskı, Beta Basım Yayım, 1998.

Yavuz, C. Borçlar Hukuku Özel Hükümler *(Obligations Law Specific Provisions),* İstanbul: Beta Basım Yayın, 1996.

Yenerer, Ö.C. Tıbbi Müdahaleye Rızanın Ceza Hukuku Açısından İncelenmesi *(Examination of Consent with Regard to Criminal Law),* Istanbul: Legal Yayıncılık, Birinci Baskı, Ocak, 2003.

Yenisey, F. & A. Nuhoğlu. Geçiş Dönemi Temel Ceza Kanunları (TCK) *(Fundamental Criminal Laws in the Intermediary Period).* İstanbul: Beta Basım A.Ş., 2005.

Yıldırım, N. Tanzimattan Cumhuriyete Koruyucu Sağlık Hizmetleri *(Preventive Health Care Services from Tanzimat to the Republic).* Tanzimattan Cumhuriyete Türkiye Ansiklopedisi, İletişim Yayınları, ss 1320–1338, 1986.

Selected Bibliography

Index

The numbers here refer to paragraph numbers.

www.ingramcontent.com/pod-product-compliance
Ingram Content Group UK Ltd.
Pitfield, Milton Keynes, MK11 3LW, UK
UKHW020146290926
15471UKWH00004B/718

9 789403 523460